MATHEMATICS

Grade 1 • Student Edition

Second Edition

purposeful design
p u b l i c a t i o n s

Colorado Springs, Colorado

Printed in the United States of America
25 24 23 22   6 7 8 9

Mathematics, Grade 1 – Student Edition
Purposeful Design Mathematics series
ISBN 978-1-58331-577-4, Catalog #40011

Purposeful Design Publications is the publishing division of the Association of Christian Schools International (ACSI) and is committed to the ministry of Christian school education, to enable Christian educators and schools worldwide to effectively prepare students for life. As the publisher of textbooks, trade books, and other educational resources within ACSI, Purposeful Design Publications strives to produce biblically sound materials that reflect Christian scholarship and stewardship and that address the identified needs of Christian schools around the world.

References to books, computer software, and other ancillary resources in this series are not endorsements by ACSI. These materials were selected to provide teachers with additional resources appropriate to the concepts being taught and to promote student understanding and enjoyment.

Images containing only money courtesy of US Mint or US Treasury.

Purposeful Design Publications
A Division of ACSI
731 Chapel Hills Drive • Colorado Springs, CO 80920
800/367-0798 • www.purposefuldesign.com

Table of Contents

He determines the number of the stars and calls them each by name. Psalm 147:4

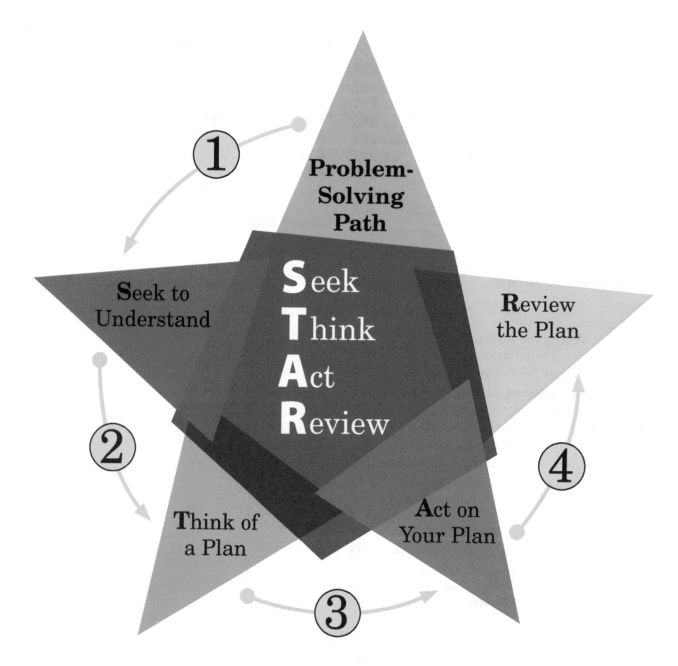

Seek to Understand

Think of a Plan

Act on Your Plan

Review the Plan

Chapter 1
Getting Started

There is the sea, vast and spacious, teeming with creatures beyond number—living things both large and small.
Psalm 104:25

Key Ideas:

Patterns: identifying sets

Patterns: classifying patterns

Numbers: skip counting, odd and even numbers

Writing: numerals 0–20

Count the crab's legs and claws. Fill in the blanks.

The crab has ---------------- legs. It has ---------------- claws.

Complete each exercise. Draw and color.

1. My favorite number is ____.

_____

- - - - - - - - - - - - - -

_____

2. I have ____ people in my family.

_____

- - - - - - - - - - - - - -

_____

Me

3. I have ____ pets.

_____

- - - - - - - - - -

_____

4. I am ____ years old.

_____

- - - - - - - - - -

_____

5. I lost ____ teeth.

_____

- - - - - - - - - -

_____

Complete each exercise. Color.

6. I have _____ letters in my first name.

_____

- - - - - - - - - - - - - - -

_____

7. I have _____ books in my desk.

_____

- - - - - - - - - - - - - -

_____

8. My house number is _____.

_____

- -

_____

9. I am in 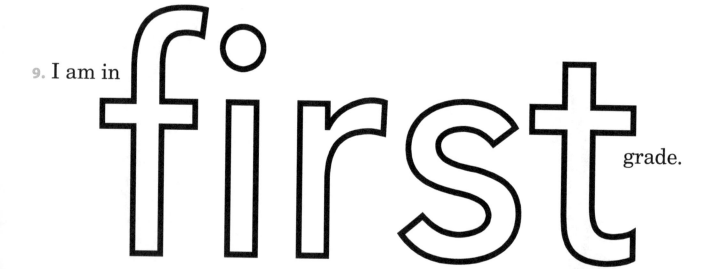 grade.

10. I was born in the year _____.

_____

- -

_____

11. A phone number I know is _____.

_____

- -

_____

12. When I am a grown-up, I will be _____ years old.

_____

- - - - - - - - - - - - - - - - -

_____

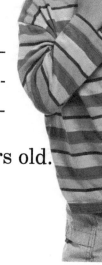

A set is a group of things that are alike in some way.

Cut out the shapes. Sort the shapes by color to make two sets. Glue the shapes in place.

1.

2.

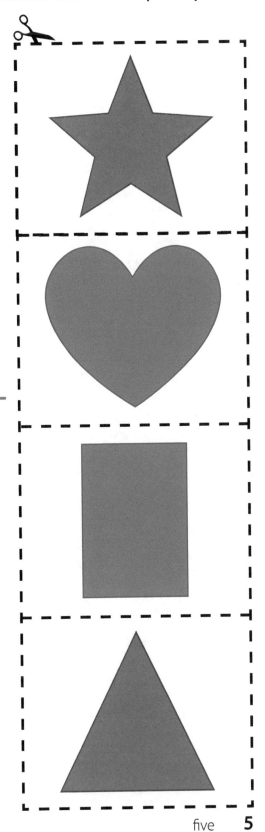

3. Trace the gray line. Circle two more sets of seashells.

1. Sort the boats by size. The first one is done for you.

2. Circle the striped fish to put in the aquarium.

Make an X on the animals that do not belong in the set.

3.

fins

4.

legs

5.

fur

6.

shell

A pattern is a series that repeats itself over and over.

Cut out the pictures at the bottom of the page. Glue in place to complete each pattern.

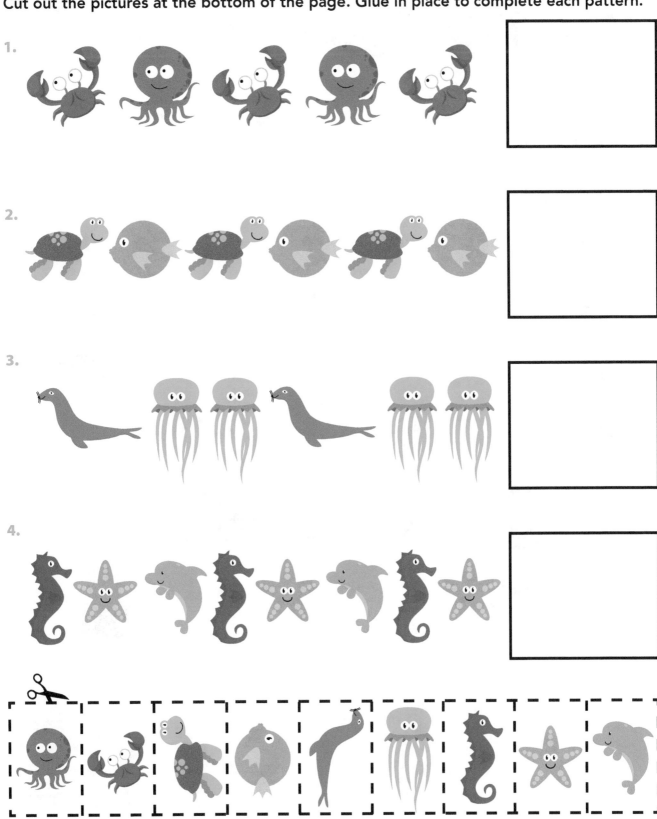

Color to continue the pattern.

5.

6.

Review

7. Circle three sets.

Choose two colors of cubes. Make a pattern. Color your pattern below.

1.

Make two different patterns using the cubes. Color your patterns below. Write the labels for your patterns.

2.

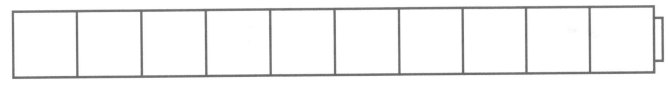

_____ _____ _____ _____ _____ _____ _____ _____

3.

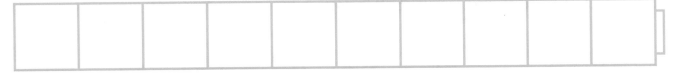

_____ _____ _____ _____ _____ _____ _____ _____

4. Read the pattern. Then read the same pattern using the letter names A, B, and C.

A   B   C   A   B   C

5. Use the letters A and B to write this pattern.

___   ___   ___   ___   ___   ___

6. Use the letters A and B to write this pattern.

___   ___   ___   ___   ___   ___

7. Use the letters A, B, and C to write this pattern.

___   ___   ___   ___   ___   ___

8. Use the letters A, B, and C to write this pattern.

___   ___   ___   ___   ___   ___   ___   ___

A **number** is a word that tells how many.

1. **Look at the picture. Count the fish. How many fish did you count?** _____

A **numeral** is a symbol that stands for a number.

Circle the numeral for each kind of fish in the picture.

2.

0 1 2 3 4

4.

0 1 2 3 4

3.

0 1 2 3 4

5.

0 1 2 3 4

Count the fish. Circle each set where the number of fish matches the numeral.

6.

3

8.

4

7.

5

9.

2

10. Draw and color a set with the same number as shown.

11. Draw and color a set with one more circle.

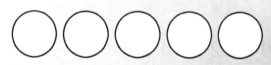

12. Draw and color a set with one less square.

Name _____

1. Write the numerals.

zero 0 0 0

one 1 1 1

two 2 2 2

three 3 3 3

2. Trace each numeral with a crayon.

1 3 2 0 0

3 2 0 1 3

Count. Write the numeral that tells the number of beans in each set.

3.

_____
- - - - - - - - - - - - - - -
_____

4.

_____
- - - - - - - - - - - - - - -
_____

5.

_____
- - - - - - - - - - - - - - -
_____

6.

_____
- - - - - - - - - - - - - - -
_____

Write tally marks for each set of beans.

7.

_____

8.

_____

9.

_____

10.

_____

11.

_____

Write tally marks for each set of pennies.

12.

_____

13.

_____

14.

_____

15. Write a tally mark for each fish.

_____

1. Write the numerals.

four

five

six

2. Trace each numeral with a crayon.

3. Write the numerals 1 through 6.

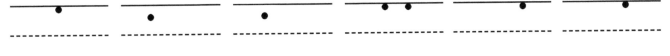

Count the beans. Write the numeral that tells the number.

4.

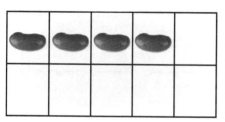

_____

_____

5.

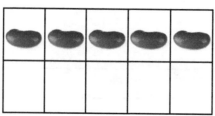

_____

_____

6.

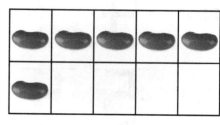

_____

_____

Count the items. Write the numeral 4, 5, or 6.

7.

_____

_____

8.

_____

_____

9.

_____

_____

Count the items. Match the numeral and number word to the correct set.

10.

four 4 •

11.

six 6 •

1. Write the numerals.

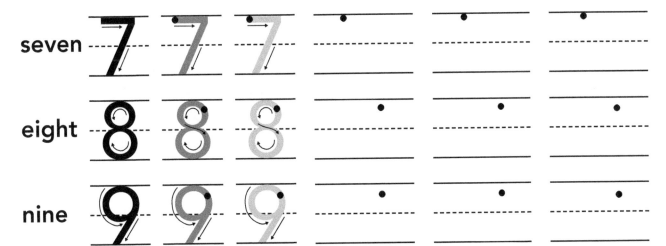

seven

eight

nine

2. Trace each numeral with a crayon.

3. Make a tally mark for each fish.

_____

4. Write the numeral that tells how many fish.

_____

- - - - - - - - - - - - -

_____

Count the beans. Write the numeral that tells the number of beans.

5.

bean	bean	bean	bean	bean
bean	bean			

———————

- - - - - - - - - - - - - - -

———————

6.

bean	bean	bean	bean	bean
bean	bean	bean		

———————

- - - - - - - - - - - - - - -

———————

7.

bean	bean	bean	bean	bean
bean	bean	bean	bean	

———————

- - - - - - - - - - - - - - -

———————

Match the set to the number word.

8. **9.** **10.**

· · ·

eight ·   seven ·   · nine

11. Draw a set of 8 ⋈.

12. Draw a set of 8 ⋈. Then draw 2 more.

13. Which bowl has more fish? Circle it.

1. Write the numerals.

ten

eleven

twelve

2. Color the cubes to match the number word.

twelve

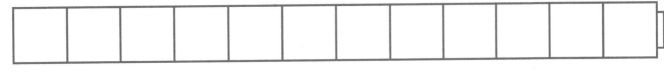

ten

eleven

3. Color 12 fish.

Count on. Trace the gray numerals. Write the missing numerals.

4. 1 2 __ 4 __ __ 7

5. 6 7 __ __ 10

6. 8 __ __ 11 12

7. Match the set to the number word.

twelve ·   eleven ·   · ten

Count the beans and write the numeral.

8.   9. 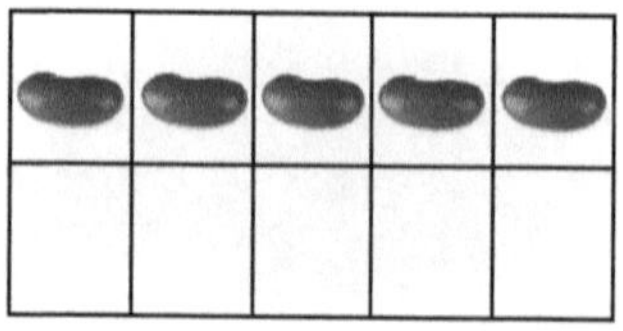   10. 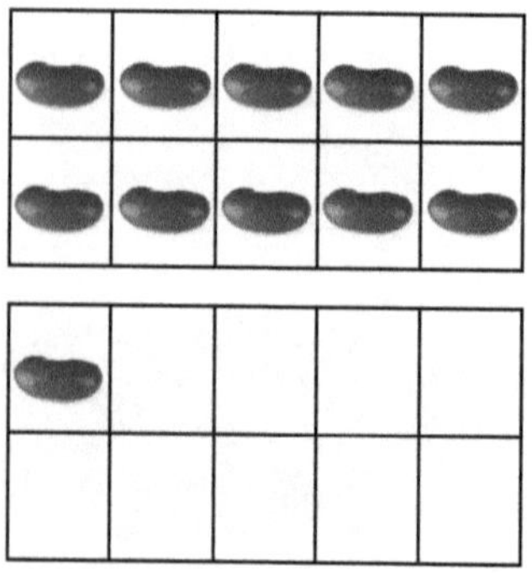   11.

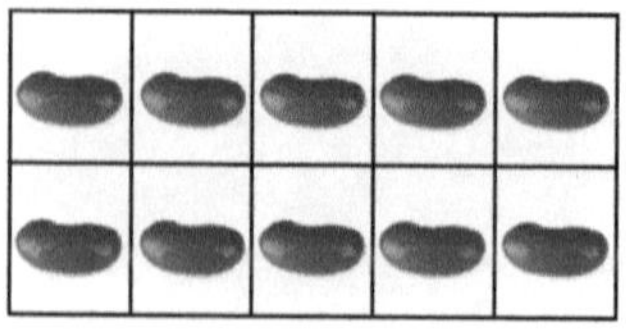

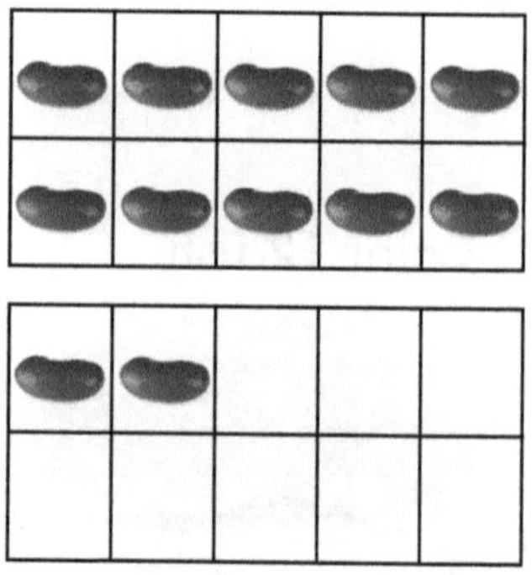

_____   _____   _____   _____

1. Count the shells. Write the numerals as you count.

2. Color the shells that are less than 10 yellow.

3. Color the shells that are 10 or more orange.

Write the numeral that tells the number in each set. Circle the set that has the largest number.

4.

5.

6.

Write the missing numerals.

7. 7 ___ ___ 10

9. 4 ___ ___ 7

8. ___ 10 ___ 12

10. 8 ___ 10 ___

Count the items. Write the numerals. Circle the set with more than 11 items.

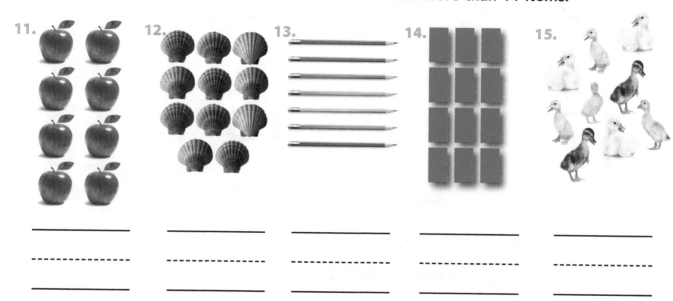

11.

12.

13.

14.

15.

Sequence, Even, and Odd 1.12

Write the numeral that comes after the one shown.

1.  _____

3.  _____

2.  _____

4.  _____

Write the numeral that comes before the one shown.

5. _____

7. _____

6. _____

8. _____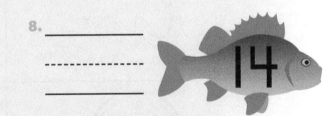

Write the numeral that comes between the ones shown.

9.  _____

10. _____

Even numbers can be divided into sets of two with no leftovers.

Odd numbers cannot be divided into sets of two without a leftover.

Circle groups of 2. The first one is done for you. Color the items in exercises that show an even number.

11.

15.

12.

16.

13.

17.

14.

18.

Use the ten-frames to count to 20.

1	2	3	4	5
6	7	8	9	10
11	12	13	14	15
16	17	18	19	20

Start at 20. Count back the number shown. Write the numeral.

1. Count back 2. ---- 18

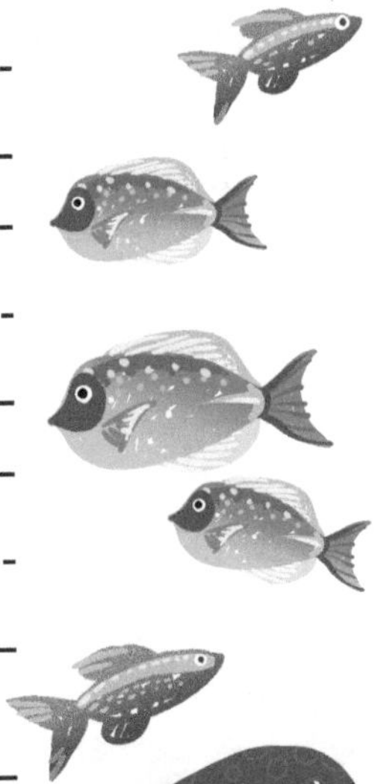

2. Count back 3. ----

3. Count back 4. ----

4. Count back 5. ----

5. Count back 6. ----

6. Count back 7. ----

7. Count back 8. ----

8. Count back 9. ----

Use the number line to count back. Write the numeral.

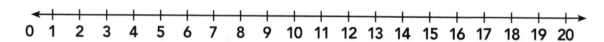

9. **20, 19, 18,** ------------------

10. **17, 16, 15,** ------------------

11. **19, 18, 17,** ------------------

12. **6, 5, 4,** ------------------

13. **16, 15, 14,** ------------------

14. **10, 9, 8,** ------------------

15. **13, 12, 11,** ------------------

16. **14, 13, 12,** ------------------

17. The fishbowl had 12 fish. Four were taken out.

Count back. Draw the correct number of fish in the fishbowl now.

1. Make an AB pattern. Color the pattern that you made.

2. Color an ABC pattern.

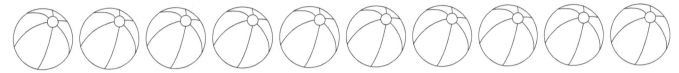

Finish the patterns.

3.

4.

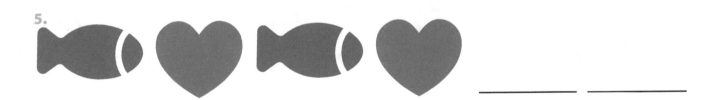

5.

Write the numeral that comes before, after, or in between the numerals shown.

6. _____ 7   7. _____ 11   8. _____ 16

9. 3 _____   10. 19 _____   11. 15 _____

12. 18 _____ 20   13. 13 _____ 15

Count the pennies.

14. _____ ¢

15. _____ ¢

16. Color the set with the even number of squares.

Chapter 2
Shapes, Sets, and Counting

I praise You because I am fearfully
and wonderfully made;
Your works are wonderful,
I know that full well.
Psalm 139:14

Key Ideas:

Geometry: plane figures–rectangle, square, triangle, hexagon, trapezoid, rhombus, circle, oval

Geometry: shape reflection, shape translation, shape rotation

Patterns: skip counting

Patterns: patterns in counting

Find and circle:

A purple rectangle
An orange circle
An orange triangle

A blue triangle
A pink star
A pink triangle

Rectangle, Triangle, Hexagon 2.1

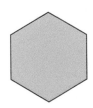

rectangle   square   triangle   hexagon

1. Draw pictures to complete the table.

shape	picture
A rectangle is a shape with four sides and four square corners.	
A square is a rectangle with four sides that are all the same length.	
A triangle is a shape with three sides.	
A hexagon is a shape with six sides.	

2. Color an AB pattern.

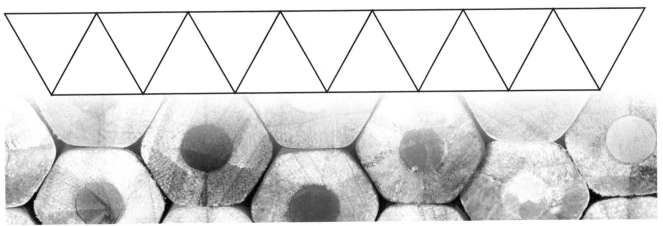

3. Color. Use the colors in the box below.

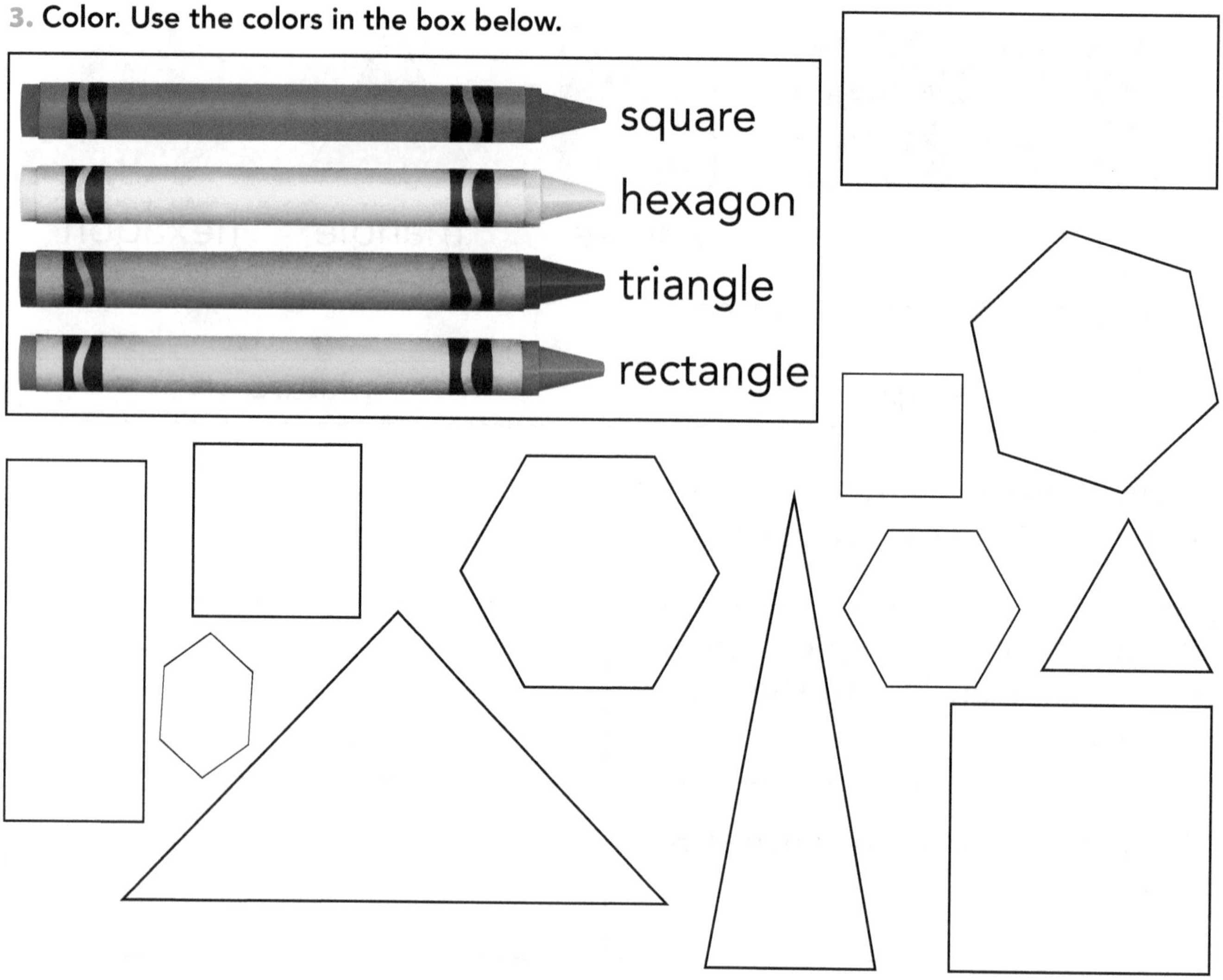

square

hexagon

triangle

rectangle

4. Color each row of shapes in a pattern. Label the patterns.

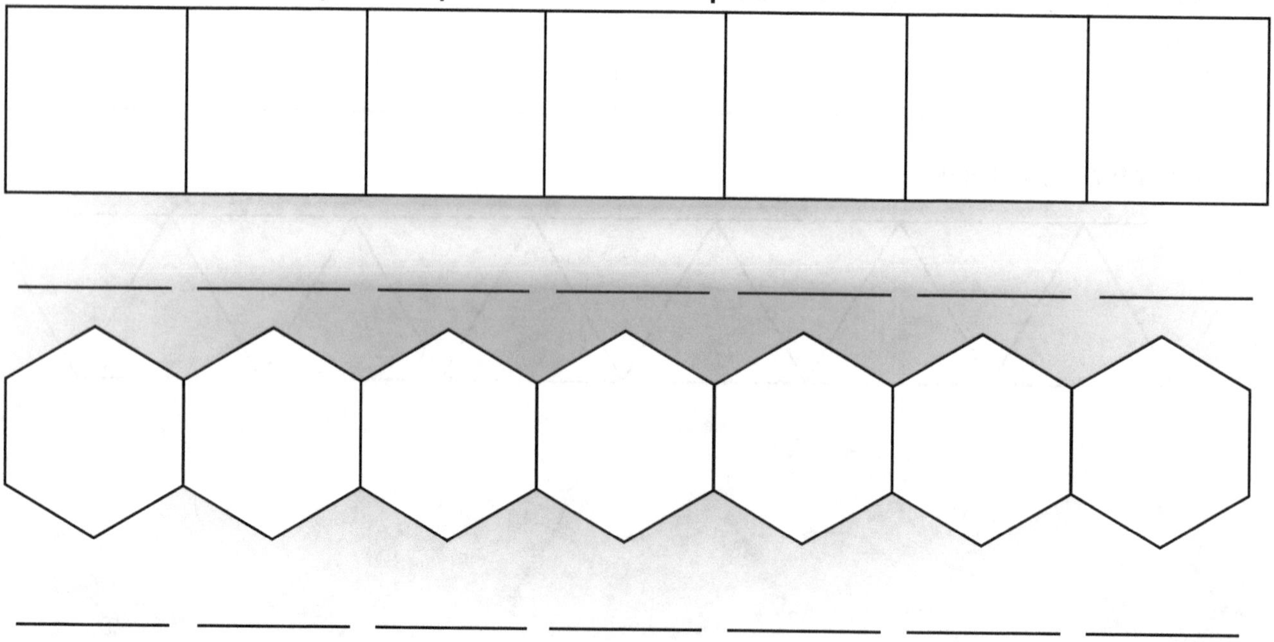

1. Say the name of each shape. Count the sides.

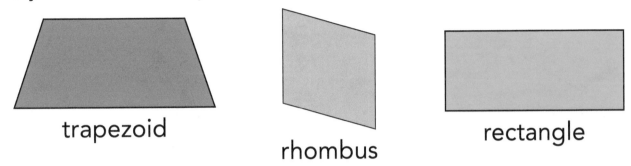

trapezoid

rhombus

rectangle

Trapezoids, rhombuses, and rectangles all have four sides. A trapezoid is a four-sided figure with no more than two slanted sides. Rhombuses have four equal sides and may have square corners. Rectangles have straight sides and four square corners.

2. Trace the shapes with a crayon. Tell the name of each shape.

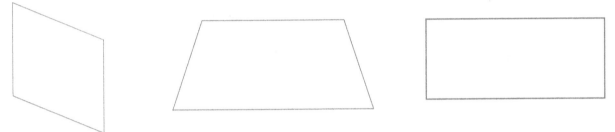

3. Complete the pattern. Use letters to label the pattern.

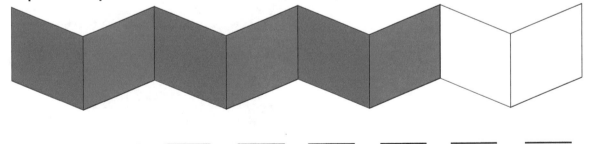

___ ___ ___ ___ ___ ___ ___ ___

4. Cover each shape with pattern blocks.

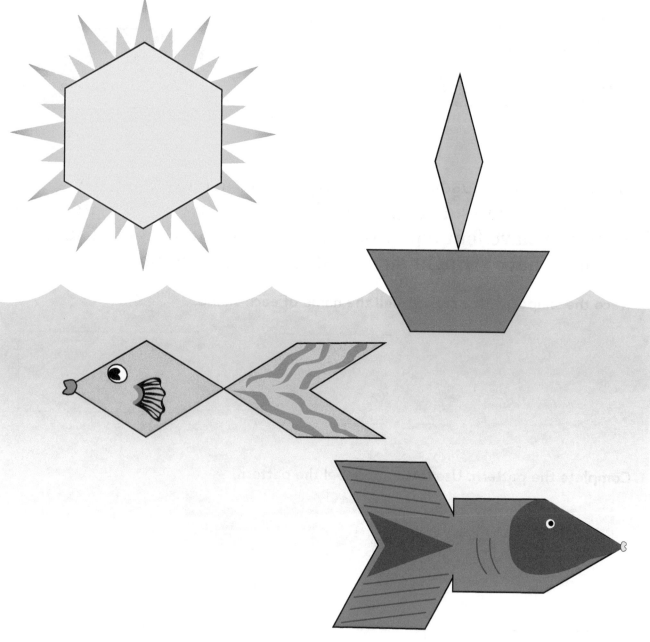

5. Tally the pattern blocks you used.

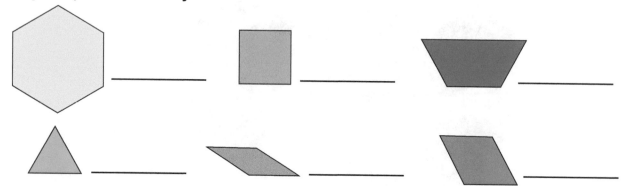

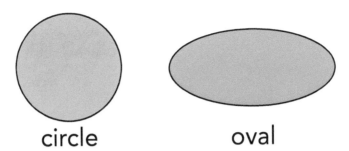

circle   oval

A circle is a perfectly round shape. The distance from the middle of the circle to the outside edge is always the same.

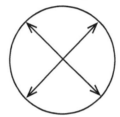

An oval is long in one direction and short in another.

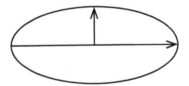

1. Color to complete the pattern.

2. Draw shapes to complete the AB pattern.

3. Trace the shapes. Color the graph to show the number of shapes in the picture.

Shapes

hexagon ⬡							
square ■							
rectangle ▬							
triangle ▲							
rhombus ▰							
trapezoid ⬭							
oval ⬬							
circle ●							

open figure

closed figure

Draw a square around the closed figures.

1.

4.

7.

2.

5.

8.

3.

6.

9.

Change the open figure to a closed figure.

10.   11.   12.

Redraw each closed figure and make it an open figure.

13.   14.

15. Draw a face. Use red to draw the closed figures on the face and blue to draw the open figures on the face.

1. Draw to show shape reflection.

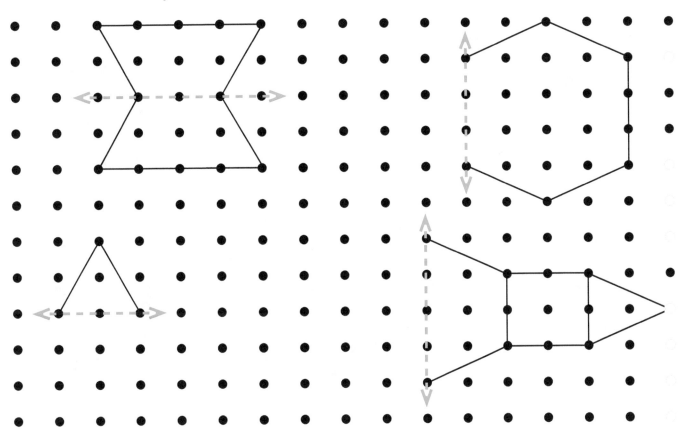

Use a mirror to see the whole picture.

2.

3.

4.

5.

Draw a line of symmetry.

6.

9.

12.

7.

10.

13.

8.

11.

14.

How many lines of symmetry can you find?

15.

16.

17.

_____

_____

_____

Shape Translation 2.6

Circle the one that is the same.

1.

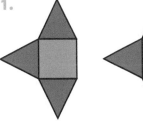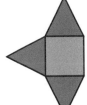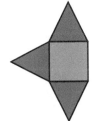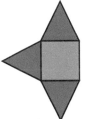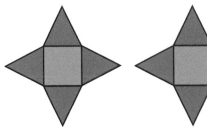

2.

3.

Cross out all the ones that are not exactly the same.

4.

5.

6.

Circle the pattern that shows shape translation.

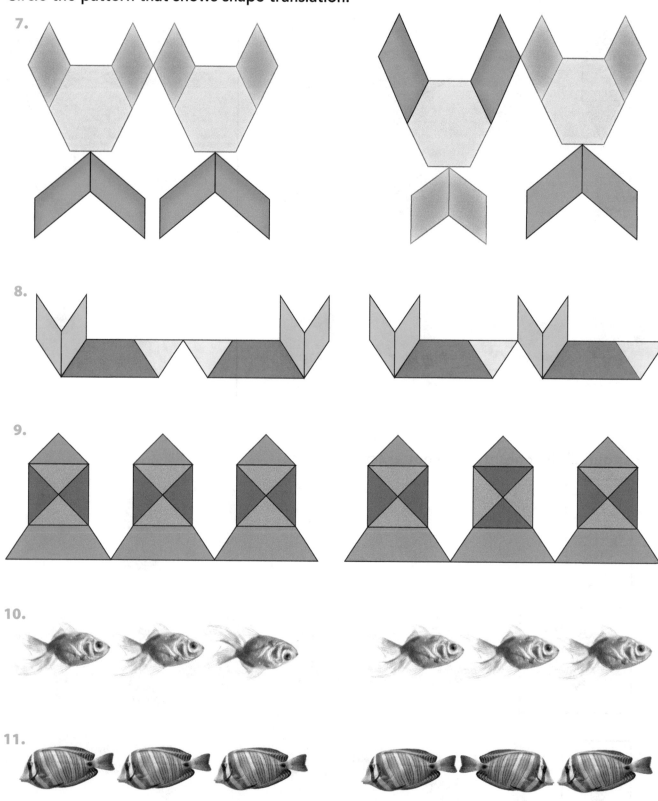

7.

8.

9.

10.

11.

Cut out the shapes. Turn them to show shape rotation. Glue them in place.

1.

3.

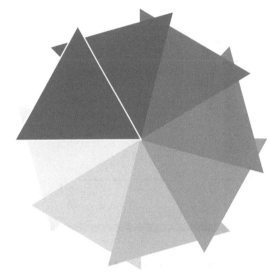

2.

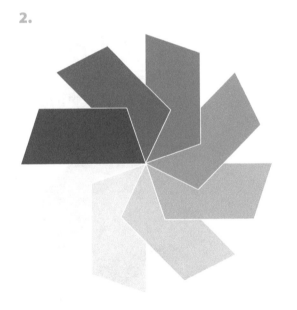

4.

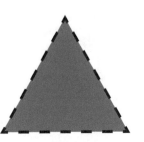

What letter has been spun or rotated?

5.    6.   7.   8.   9.

_____ _____ _____ _____ _____

Review

10. Circle the sea creatures that show shape reflection. Draw the line of symmetry.

Name _____

Equal means having the same number.

Count the number in each set. Write the numeral. Circle sets that have an equal number of objects.

1.       3.

_____   _____   _____   _____

2.    4.

_____   _____   _____   _____

5. Draw starfish to make the sets show an equal number. Write the equals sign = on the line.

   _____

6. Color two equal sets of connecting cubes.

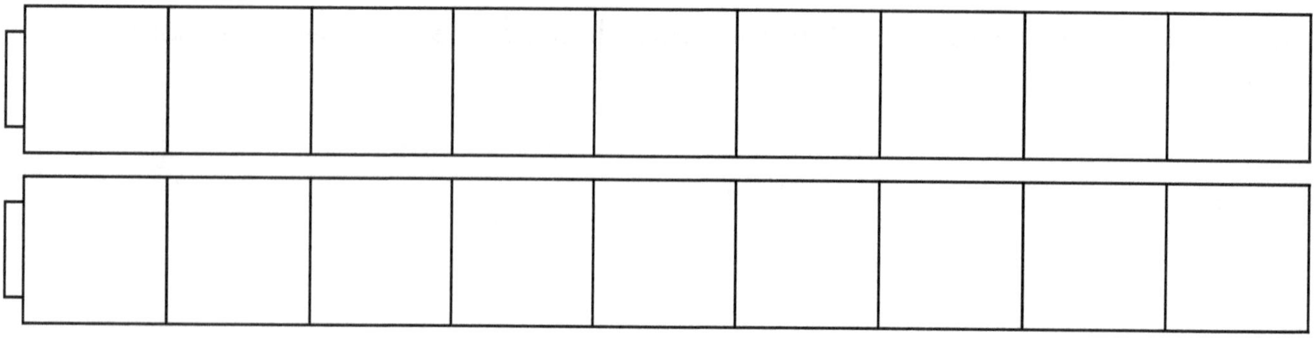

Review

Name the shapes. Circle the two sets in each row that have an equal number of shapes.

7.

8.

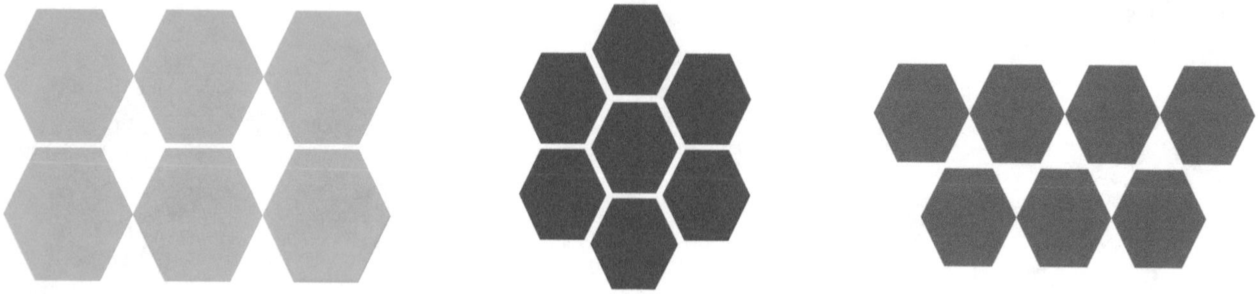

9.

1. The animals are leaving the ark. Count them by 2s. Write the numerals.

_____   _____   _____   _____

_____   _____   _____   _____

_____   _____   _____   _____

2. Color the numbers that you say when you count by 2s.

Hundred Chart

1	2	3	4	5	6	7	8	9	10
11	12	13	14	15	16	17	18	19	20
21	22	23	24	25	26	27	28	29	30
31	32	33	34	35	36	37	38	39	40
41	42	43	44	45	46	47	48	49	50
51	52	53	54	55	56	57	58	59	60
61	62	63	64	65	66	67	68	69	70
71	72	73	74	75	76	77	78	79	80
81	82	83	84	85	86	87	88	89	90
91	92	93	94	95	96	97	98	99	100

3. Circle groups of 2. Count by 2s. How many frogs are there in all? _____

Name _____

1. Count the starfish arms by 5s. Write the numerals.

_____   _____   _____   _____

_____   _____   _____   _____

_____   _____   _____   _____

2. Count the tallies by 5s. Write the numerals.

 = _____    = _____

 = _____    = _____

3. Color the numbers that you say when you count by 5s.

Hundred Chart

1	2	3	4	5	6	7	8	9	10
11	12	13	14	15	16	17	18	19	20
21	22	23	24	25	26	27	28	29	30
31	32	33	34	35	36	37	38	39	40
41	42	43	44	45	46	47	48	49	50
51	52	53	54	55	56	57	58	59	60
61	62	63	64	65	66	67	68	69	70
71	72	73	74	75	76	77	78	79	80
81	82	83	84	85	86	87	88	89	90
91	92	93	94	95	96	97	98	99	100

Count the nickels. Write the amount.

4. = _____ ¢

5. = _____ ¢

6. = _____ ¢

penny = 1¢ ——————→ count by 1s

 nickel = 5¢ ——————→ count by 5s

 dime = 10¢ ——————→ count by 10s

Count the coins. Write the amount.

1.

      = _____ ¢

2.

       = _____ ¢

3.

      = _____ ¢

4. Circle the set that has the greater value.

5. Count the number in one row. Match the counting pattern.

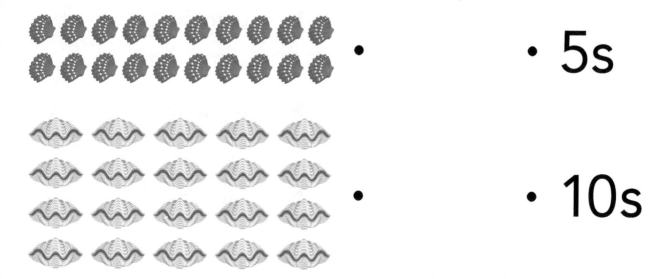

•   • 5s

•   • 10s

6. Count by 2s. Begin at 0.

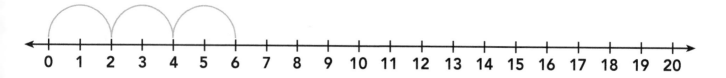

7. Count by 5s. Begin at 0.

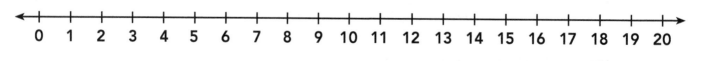

8. Count by 10s. Begin at 0.

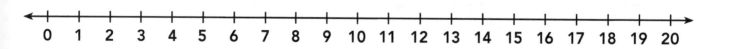

1. Write the missing numerals.

Hundred Chart

1	2	3		5	6		8	9	10
11		13	14	15	16	17		19	20
21	22		24		26	27	28	29	30
	32	33		35			38	39	
41	42	43	44	45		47	48		50
51		53		55	56		58	59	60
	62		64		66		68	69	70
71	72	73		75		77		79	80
81		83		85		87	88	89	90
91	92	93	94		96		98	99	100

Color the hundred chart.

2. Color the boxes

to show even numbers.

3. Outline the boxes in

to show counting by 10s.

Hundred Chart

1	2	3	4	5	6	7	8	9	10
11	12	13	14	15	16	17	18	19	20
21	22	23	24	25	26	27	28	29	30
31	32	33	34	35	36	37	38	39	40
41	42	43	44	45	46	47	48	49	50
51	52	53	54	55	56	57	58	59	60
61	62	63	64	65	66	67	68	69	70
71	72	73	74	75	76	77	78	79	80
81	82	83	84	85	86	87	88	89	90
91	92	93	94	95	96	97	98	99	100

Complete the number patterns.

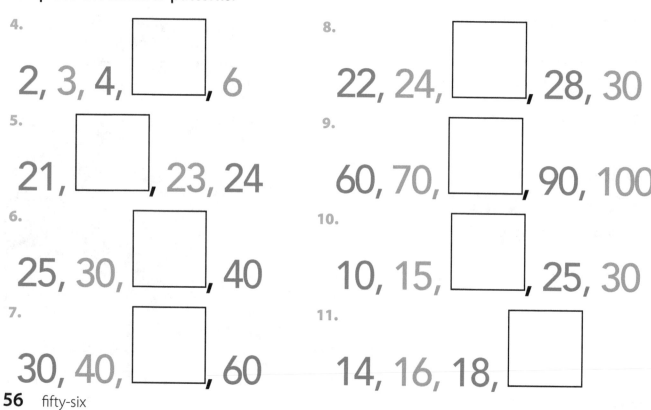

4. 2, 3, 4, ☐, 6

8. 22, 24, ☐, 28, 30

5. 21, ☐, 23, 24

9. 60, 70, ☐, 90, 100

6. 25, 30, ☐, 40

10. 10, 15, ☐, 25, 30

7. 30, 40, ☐, 60

11. 14, 16, 18, ☐

Ordinal Numbers 2.13

1st, 2nd, 3rd, 4th, 5th, 6th, 7th, 8th, 9th, 10th

first second third fourth fifth sixth seventh eighth ninth tenth

Color.

1. third

   sixth

2. first

   tenth

3. eighth

   seventh

4. second

   fifth

5. fourth

   ninth

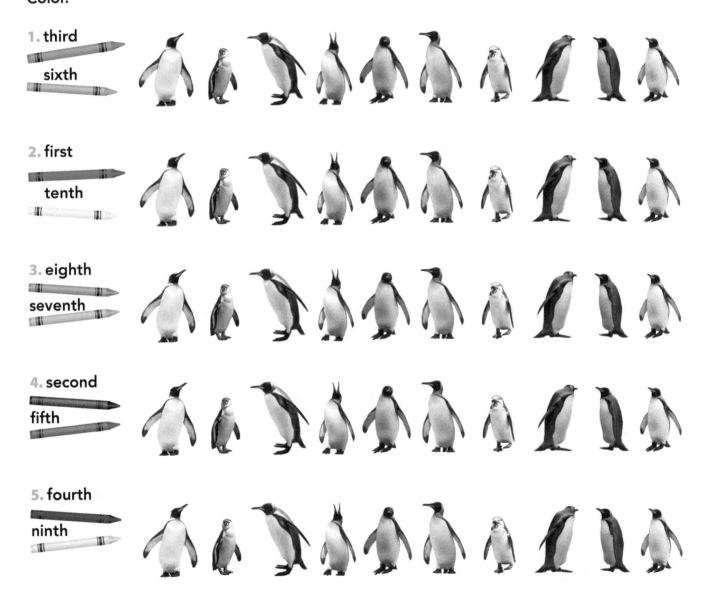

Look at the picture. Answer the questions.

6. Becky is ninth in line. Ken is seventh in line. Noah is between them. Which place is Noah in?

_____

7. Jo is buying some tickets. She is after the third person. Which place is Jo in?

_____

8. Collin and Logan are in line for recess. They have two people between them. Logan is second. Which place is Collin in?

_____

9. Draw a hat on the third child in line. Draw a flower in the hand of the sixth child in line.

10. Put a blue X below the first child in line. Draw a green circle around the tenth child.

Hundred Chart

1	2	3	4	5	6	7	8	9	10
11	12	13	14	15	16	17	18	19	20
21	22	23	24	25	26	27	28	29	30
31	32	33	34	35	36	37	38	39	40
41	42	43	44	45	46	47	48	49	50
51	52	53	54	55	56	57	58	59	60
61	62	63	64	65	66	67	68	69	70
71	72	73	74	75	76	77	78	79	80
81	82	83	84	85	86	87	88	89	90
91	92	93	94	95	96	97	98	99	100

1. Count by fives. Color each number yellow.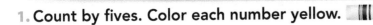

2. Count by tens. Outline each number in blue.

3. Circle other patterns you can find. Use different colors.

Use the chart. Fill in the missing number.

4. 44, _____, 46

5. _____, 39, 40

6. 27, _____, 29

7. 14, 15, _____

8. 85, _____, 87

9. 98, 99, _____

Use the hundred chart.

10. What is 3 more than 10? _____

11. What is 2 more than 63? _____

12. What is 5 more than 15? _____

13. What is 4 less than 56? _____

14. What is 1 less than 99? _____

15. What is 7 less than 87? _____

16. Look at your answers above. Write the lowest number on the first line below. Fill in the rest of the spaces.

_____ _____ _____ _____ _____ _____

    first   second   third   fourth   fifth   sixth

17. Is the third number higher or lower than 50? Circle your answer.

higher   lower

Circle the smaller number.

18. **48** or **84**   **21.** **89** or **79**

19. **8** or **20**   **22.** **53** or **75**

20. **12** or **11**   **23.** **30** or **20**

1. Match the shape to the number of sides.

4   6   3

2. Draw an oval.

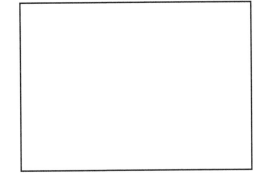

3. Circle the open figures.

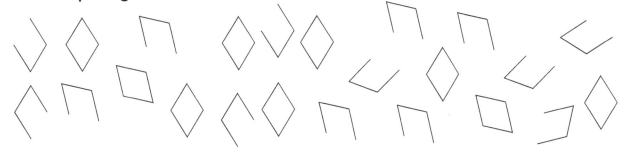

4. Circle the image with shape reflection.

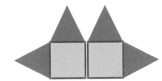

5. Continue the pattern to show shape translation.

 _____ _____ _____ _____ _____

6. What letter has been spun?

 _____

Fill in the missing numbers.

7. 20, _____, 22

9. 81, _____, 85, 87

8. 30, _____, 50, 60, _____

Count the money.

10.     = _____ ¢

11.   = _____ ¢

12.   = _____ ¢

13. **Cross out the fourth starfish.**

14. **Color the first triangle blue and the tenth triangle orange.**

 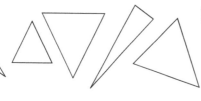 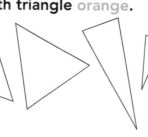 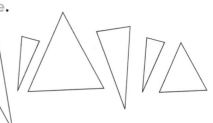

15. **Circle the sets that are equal in number.**

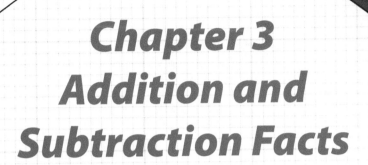

Chapter 3
Addition and
Subtraction Facts

Great are the works of the Lord;
they are pondered by all who
delight in them.
Psalm 111:2

Key Ideas:

Addition: basic facts to 12, doubles, using three addends

Subtraction: basic facts to 12

Algebra: writing number sentences

Add the objects in the picture.

2 🌴 plus 2 🩴 equals ____.

1 🏐 plus 2 🏄 equals ____.

1 ☀️ plus 1 🐚 equals ____.

When you put two numbers together, you **add**. Each number added is an **addend**. The result of adding is the **sum**. The word plus means added to, and a plus sign is a symbol used for addition.

addend → 2 + 3 = 5 ← sum
addend → plus sign

Write the addends. Trace the plus sign.

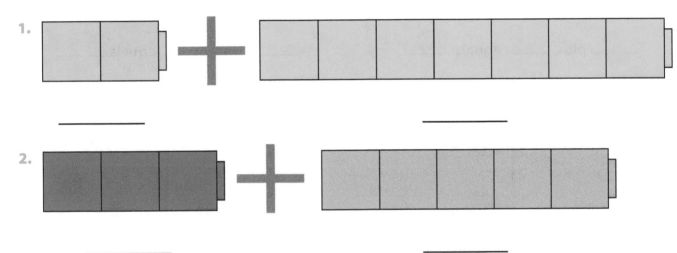

1. _____   _____

2. _____   _____

Write a number sentence to match each picture.

3. ___ + ___ = ___

6. ___ + ___ = ___

4. ___ + ___ = ___

7. ___ + ___ = ___

5. ___ + ___ = ___

8. ___ + ___ = ___

Write the numerals. Complete the number sentences. The first exercise is done for you.

9.
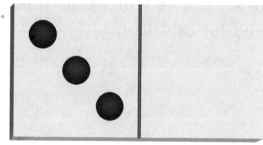

$\underline{3}$ plus $\underline{0}$ equals $\underline{3}$.

12.
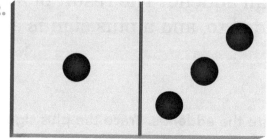

_____ plus _____ equals _____.

10.

_____ plus _____ equals _____.

13.
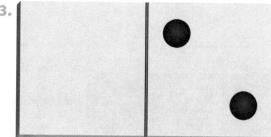

_____ plus _____ equals _____.

11.
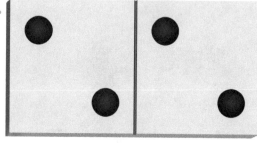

_____ plus _____ equals _____.

14.
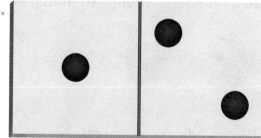

_____ plus _____ equals _____.

15. Tess has 2 shells.   Jim has 5 shells.   How many shells in all?

Write the addends. Trace the + and = signs. Write the sum.

_____ + _____ = _____

You can count on to add. The number you start with is an addend. The number you count on is an addend. The number you land on is the sum.

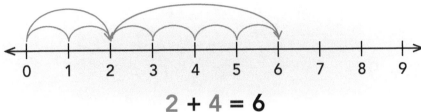

2 + 4 = 6

Count the hops. Write the addends.

1.
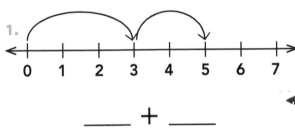

_____ + _____

2.
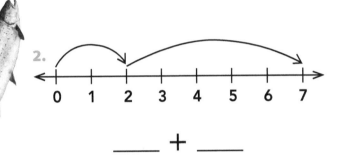

_____ + _____

Complete the number sentences.

3.
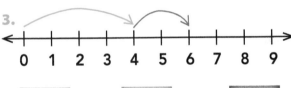

☐ + ☐ = ☐

5.
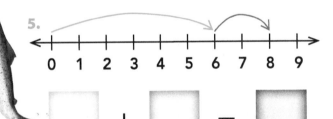

☐ + ☐ = ☐

4.
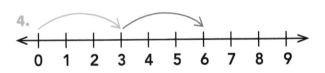

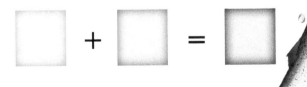

☐ + ☐ = ☐

6.
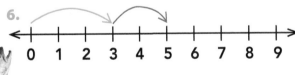

☐ + ☐ = ☐

7. Use the number line to count on. Write the sums.

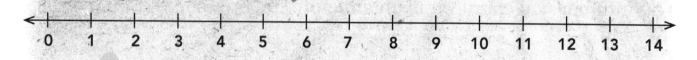

1 + 5 = ____   0 + 3 = ____

2 + 0 = ____   3 + 1 = ____

3 + 3 = ____   2 + 3 = ____

4 + 2 = ____   1 + 1 = ____

Count on. Write the sums.

8.

   + 2 = ____

9.

   + 5 = ____

10.

   + 3 = ____

Introducing Subtraction

To subtract means to take away. When you subtract, you find how many are left. Minus means to subtract, and a minus sign is a symbol used in subtraction.

1. Eight fish were in a bowl. One jumped into another bowl. How many are left?

Write the subtraction sentence. Solve.

☐ **–** ☐ **=** ☐ fish

2. There were 4  . A  scared 3 away.

How many fish are left?

Write the subtraction sentence. Solve.

☐ **–** ☐ **=** ☐ fish

Mark off the number subtracted. Circle and write the number left.

3.

$$6 - 1 = \underline{\quad}$$

5.

$$5 - 2 = \underline{\quad}$$

4.

$$5 - 4 = \underline{\quad}$$

6.

$$6 - 2 = \underline{\quad}$$

Write the number sentences. Subtract.

7.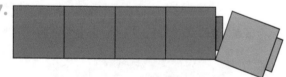

$$5 - \underline{\quad} = \underline{\quad}$$

9.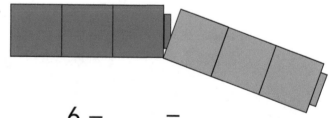

$$6 - \underline{\quad} = \underline{\quad}$$

8.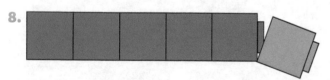

$$\underline{\quad} - \underline{\quad} = \underline{\quad}$$

10.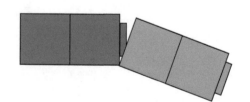

$$\underline{\quad} - \underline{\quad} = \underline{\quad}$$

Write the facts. Use only the numerals on the fish. The first one is done for you.

1.

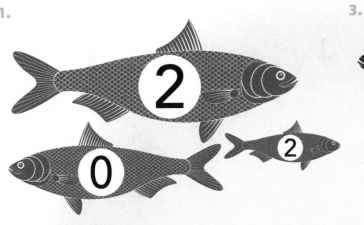

2 + 0 = 2

0 + 2 = 2

2 − 0 = 2

2 − 2 = 0

3.

___ + ___ = ___

___ − ___ = ___

2.

___ + ___ = ___

___ + ___ = ___

___ − ___ = ___

___ − ___ = ___

4.

___ + ___ = ___

___ + ___ = ___

___ − ___ = ___

___ − ___ = ___

Write the facts. Use only the numerals shown. When subtracting, start with the largest number.

5.

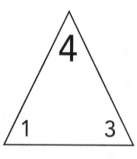

___ + ___ = ___

___ + ___ = ___

___ − ___ = ___

___ − ___ = ___

6.

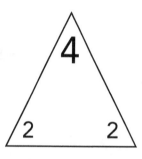

___ + ___ = ___

___ − ___ = ___

7.

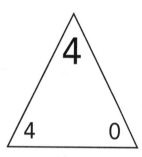

___ + ___ = ___

___ + ___ = ___

___ − ___ = ___

___ − ___ = ___

Add.

8. $1 + 3 =$ ___

9. $2 + 1 =$ ___

10. $0 + 4 =$ ___

11. $0 + 1 =$ ___

12. $3 + 1 =$ ___

Subtract.

13. $4 - 2 =$ ___

14. $3 - 1 =$ ___

15. $4 - 0 =$ ___

16. $3 - 2 =$ ___

17. $4 - 1 =$ ___

Finish the picture.

1.

3 + 2 = 5

3.

1 + 5 = 6

2.

2 + 4 = 6

4.

3 + 3 = 6

Write a number sentence.

5.

____ + ____ = ____

8.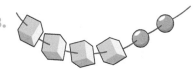

____ + ____ = ____

11.

____ + ____ = ____

6.

____ + ____ = ____

9.

____ + ____ = ____

12.

____ + ____ = ____

7.

____ + ____ = ____

10.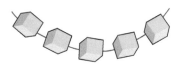

____ + ____ = ____

13.

____ + ____ = ____

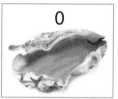

0

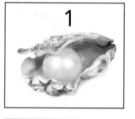

1

2

3

4

5

6

14. Write the facts for 5.

0 + 5 = ____	5 – 0 = ____
1 + 4 = ____	5 – 1 = ____
2 + 3 = ____	5 – 2 = ____
3 + 2 = ____	5 – 3 = ____
4 + 1 = ____	5 – 4 = ____
5 + 0 = ____	5 – 5 = ____

15. Write the facts for 6.

0 + 6 = ____	6 – 0 = ____
1 + 5 = ____	6 – 1 = ____
2 + 4 = ____	6 – 2 = ____
3 + 3 = ____	6 – 3 = ____
4 + 2 = ____	6 – 4 = ____
5 + 1 = ____	6 – 5 = ____
6 + 0 = ____	6 – 6 = ____

Count, write, and add.

1.
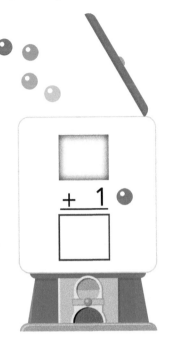

$$+ \; 1$$

2.
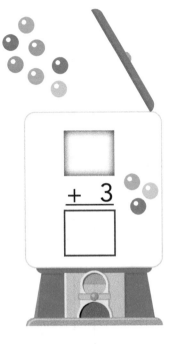

$$+ \; 3$$

3.
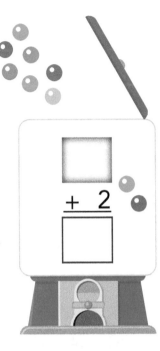

$$+ \; 2$$

Add.

4.
$$\begin{array}{r} 5 \\ + \; 1 \\ \hline \end{array}$$

7.
$$\begin{array}{r} 2 \\ + \; 3 \\ \hline \end{array}$$
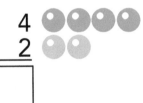

10.
$$\begin{array}{r} 2 \\ + \; 2 \\ \hline \end{array}$$
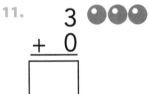

5.
$$\begin{array}{r} 1 \\ + \; 4 \\ \hline \end{array}$$

8.
$$\begin{array}{r} 4 \\ + \; 2 \\ \hline \end{array}$$

11.
$$\begin{array}{r} 3 \\ + \; 0 \\ \hline \end{array}$$

6.
$$\begin{array}{r} 2 \\ + \; 4 \\ \hline \end{array}$$

9.
$$\begin{array}{r} 3 \\ + \; 2 \\ \hline \end{array}$$

12.
$$\begin{array}{r} 2 \\ + \; 1 \\ \hline \end{array}$$
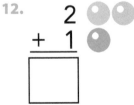

Mark off to subtract.

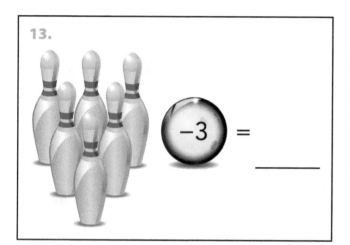

13. -3 = _____

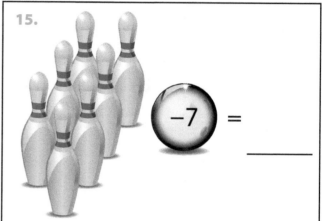

15. -7 = _____

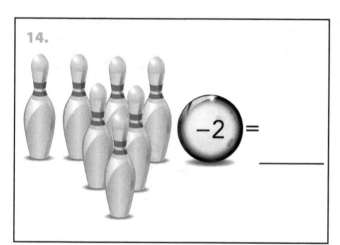

14. -2 = _____

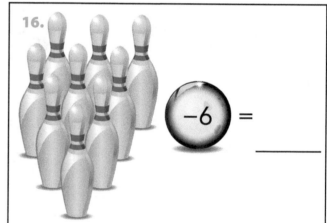

16. -6 = _____

Subtract.

17.
$$\begin{array}{r} 6 \\ -\ 5 \\ \hline \end{array}$$

18.
$$\begin{array}{r} 5 \\ -\ 4 \\ \hline \end{array}$$

19.
$$\begin{array}{r} 6 \\ -\ 2 \\ \hline \end{array}$$

20.
$$\begin{array}{r} 3 \\ -\ 2 \\ \hline \end{array}$$

Add or subtract.

21.
$$\begin{array}{r} 4 \\ -\ 2 \\ \hline \end{array}$$

22.
$$\begin{array}{r} 3 \\ +\ 3 \\ \hline \end{array}$$

23.
$$\begin{array}{r} 1 \\ +\ 4 \\ \hline \end{array}$$

24.
$$\begin{array}{r} 5 \\ -\ 2 \\ \hline \end{array}$$

Write the number sentences.

1.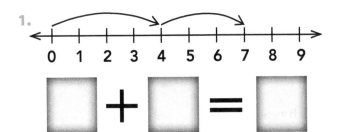

□ **+** □ **=** □

3.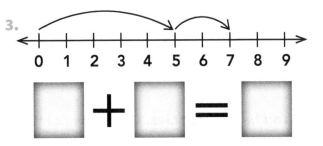

□ **+** □ **=** □

2.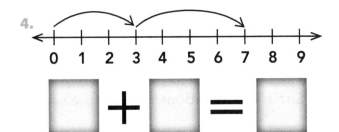

□ **+** □ **=** □

4.

□ **+** □ **=** □

Write the facts. Use only the numerals shown.

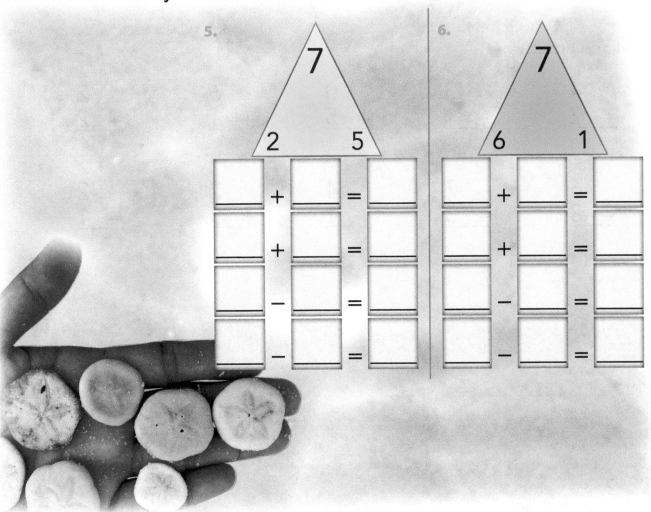

5.

7

2   5

□ + □ = □
□ + □ = □
□ − □ = □
□ − □ = □

6.

7

6   1

□ + □ = □
□ + □ = □
□ − □ = □
□ − □ = □

7. You have a nickel. Circle the coins you need to have 7 cents.

8. You have 2 pennies. Circle the coins you need to have 6 cents.

9. Circle the equations that are the same.

$$7 + 0 = 7 \qquad \begin{array}{r} 7 \\ -\ 0 \\ \hline 7 \end{array} \qquad \begin{array}{r} 5 \\ +\ 2 \\ \hline 7 \end{array} \qquad 2 + 5 = 7 \qquad 5 + 2 = 7$$

Add or subtract.

10.
$$\begin{array}{r} 4 \\ +\ 2 \\ \hline \end{array}$$

12.
$$\begin{array}{r} 3 \\ -\ 1 \\ \hline \end{array}$$

14.
$$\begin{array}{r} 0 \\ +\ 5 \\ \hline \end{array}$$

16.
$$\begin{array}{r} 6 \\ +\ 1 \\ \hline \end{array}$$

18.
$$\begin{array}{r} 2 \\ +\ 2 \\ \hline \end{array}$$

11.
$$\begin{array}{r} 6 \\ -\ 3 \\ \hline \end{array}$$

13.
$$\begin{array}{r} 7 \\ -\ 3 \\ \hline \end{array}$$

15.
$$\begin{array}{r} 4 \\ +\ 1 \\ \hline \end{array}$$

17.
$$\begin{array}{r} 2 \\ +\ 5 \\ \hline \end{array}$$

19.
$$\begin{array}{r} 2 \\ -\ 1 \\ \hline \end{array}$$

Name _____

Write the facts.

1.
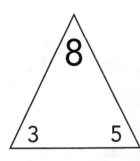

___ + ___ = ___

___ + ___ = ___

___ − ___ = ___

___ − ___ = ___

4.
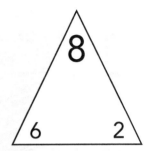

___ + ___ = ___

___ + ___ = ___

___ − ___ = ___

___ − ___ = ___

3.

___ + ___ = ___

___ + ___ = ___

___ − ___ = ___

___ − ___ = ___

2.

___ + ___ = ___

___ − ___ = ___

5.
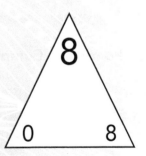

___ + ___ = ___

___ + ___ = ___

___ − ___ = ___

___ − ___ = ___

Count. Write the number sentences.

6.

7.

8.

_____ + _____ = _____   _____ + _____ = _____   _____ + _____ = _____

Use drawings, tally marks, or number sentences to show the numbers in the boxes.

9.

7

10.

8

Review

Count the money. Complete the number sentence. Draw the missing (5¢) and (1¢) coins.

11.

_____ ¢ − _____ ¢ = __3__ ¢

13.

_____ ¢ + _____ ¢ = _____ ¢

12.

_____ ¢ + _____ ¢ = __8__ ¢

14.

_____ ¢ + _____ ¢ = __7__ ¢

Name _____

1. Circle the number sentences that are equal to 9.

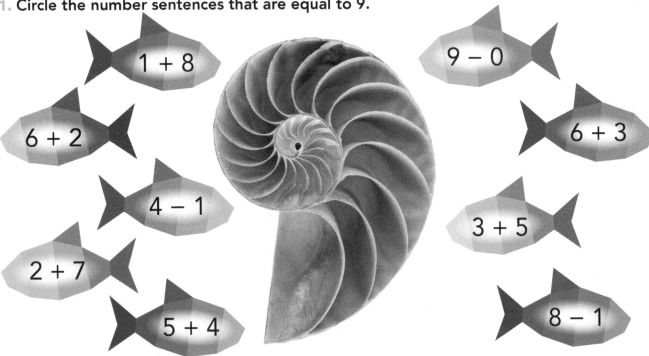

1 + 8

9 − 0

6 + 2

6 + 3

4 − 1

3 + 5

2 + 7

8 − 1

5 + 4

Mark off the coins needed to make the amounts.

2.

8¢ =

3.

9¢ =

4. Count the coconuts. If two fall off the tree, how many are left?

_____

5. Write the number sentence.

_____ + _____ = _____

Mark off to subtract.

6.

$9 - 3 = \underline{\hspace{2em}}$

8.

$9 - 6 = \underline{\hspace{2em}}$

10.

$9 - 7 = \underline{\hspace{2em}}$

7.

$9 - 5 = \underline{\hspace{2em}}$

9.

$9 - 8 = \underline{\hspace{2em}}$

11.

$9 - 4 = \underline{\hspace{2em}}$

12. **Write the missing numerals.**

 9 / 1 ____

 9 / 5 ____

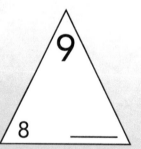 9 / 8 ____

 9 / 4 ____

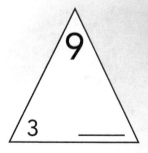 9 / 3 ____

 9 / 6 ____

 9 / 0 ____

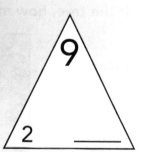 9 / 2 ____

Add.

1. 7 + [3] = _____

4. 8 + [2] = _____

2. 5 + [5] = _____

5. 4 + [5] = _____

3. 6 + [3] = _____

6. 7 + [2] = _____

7. Circle the coins needed to make the amount.

10¢ =

8. Write the missing numerals.

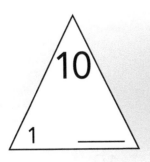

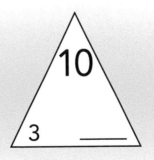

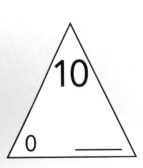

Roll a number cube. Mark off the number of pins. Complete the subtraction sentence.

9.

$10 - \underline{\qquad} = \underline{\qquad}$

11.

$10 - \underline{\qquad} = \underline{\qquad}$

13.

$10 - \underline{\qquad} = \underline{\qquad}$

10.

$10 - \underline{\qquad} = \underline{\qquad}$

12.

$10 - \underline{\qquad} = \underline{\qquad}$

14.

$10 - \underline{\qquad} = \underline{\qquad}$

Make 3 more subtraction sentences. Subtract a number 7 through 10.

15.

$10 - \underline{\qquad} = \underline{\qquad}$

16.

$10 - \underline{\qquad} = \underline{\qquad}$

17.

$10 - \underline{\qquad} = \underline{\qquad}$

Cut out the crab. Start the crab in the box for the first addend. Count on. Write the sum.

1	2	3	4	5	6	7	8	9	10	11

1. 7 + 3 = _____   5. 6 + 4 = _____   9. 2 + 7 = _____

2. 3 + 4 = _____   6. 8 + 2 = _____   10. 5 + 4 = _____

3. 6 + 3 = _____   7. 8 + 3 = _____   11. 9 + 2 = _____

4. 8 + 1 = _____   8. 5 + 6 = _____   12. 2 + 6 = _____

Add. Circle equations with sums of 12.

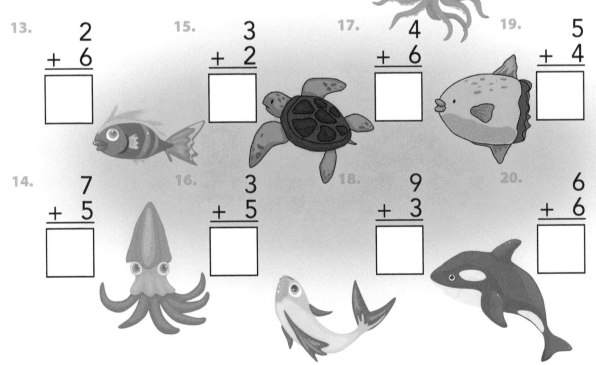

13. 2
    + 6
    [ ]

15. 3
    + 2
    [ ]

17. 4
    + 6
    [ ]

19. 5
    + 4
    [ ]

14. 7
    + 5
    [ ]

16. 3
    + 5
    [ ]

18. 9
    + 3
    [ ]

20. 6
    + 6
    [ ]

21. Add. Write the sums.

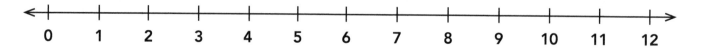

0   1   2   3   4   5   6   7   8   9   10   11   12

$0 + 1 =$ _____ $2 + 3 =$ _____ $4 + 5 =$ _____

$1 + 1 =$ _____ $4 + 2 =$ _____ $7 + 3 =$ _____

$2 + 1 =$ _____ $5 + 2 =$ _____ $6 + 5 =$ _____

$3 + 1 =$ _____ $3 + 5 =$ _____ $5 + 7 =$ _____

22. Connect the dots in the order of the sums.

The answer to a subtraction problem is the difference.

Count back to solve a subtraction problem.

1. 11 − 4 = ____. Say 11. Count back 10, 9, 8, 7.

Subtract. The dots will help you count back.

2. $\begin{array}{r} 9 \\ -\ 2 \\ \hline \end{array}$
3. $\begin{array}{r} 7 \\ -\ 3 \\ \hline \end{array}$
4. $\begin{array}{r} 5 \\ -\ 1 \\ \hline \end{array}$
5. $\begin{array}{r} 6 \\ -\ 2 \\ \hline \end{array}$

Circle count on or count back and solve the exercises.

6. 4 + 1 = _____   count on   count back

7. 8 − 2 = _____   count on   count back

8. 11 − 1 = _____   count on   count back

9. 8 + 2 = _____   count on   count back

10. **Write a subtraction sentence to match the picture. Solve.**

_____ − _____ = _____
fish that   fish that   difference
were in   jumped
the water   out

Complete the number sentences.

11.

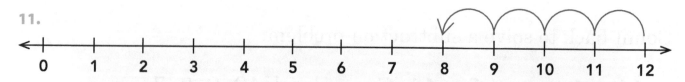

$$12 - 4 = \underline{\qquad}$$

12.

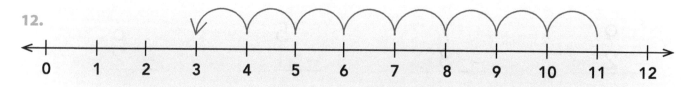

$$11 - 8 = \underline{\qquad}$$

13.

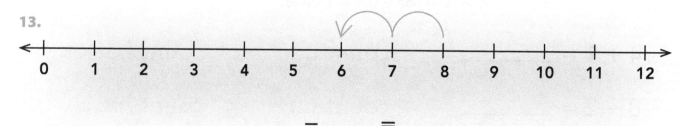

$$\underline{\qquad} - \underline{\qquad} = \underline{\qquad}$$

Draw the arrows. Complete the number sentences.

14.

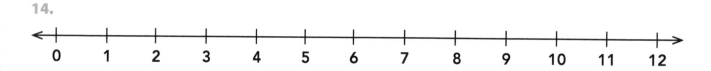

$$10 - 5 = \underline{\qquad}$$

15.

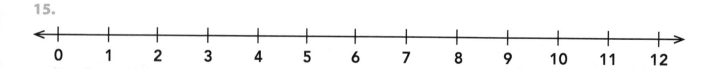

$$11 - 7 = \underline{\qquad}$$

You can add three addends. Add the first two addends. Then count on to add the third addend.

Choose three crayons of different colors. Color the beads to match the number of each addend. Count the beads to find the sum. The first one is done for you.

1. 7 + 1 + 2 = ___10___

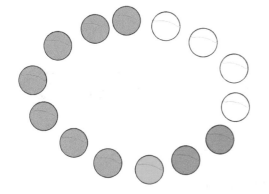

4. 2 + 6 + 1 = _____

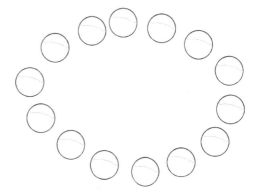

2. 5 + 4 + 2 = _____

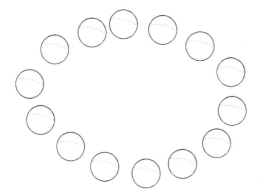

5. 8 + 1 + 0 = _____

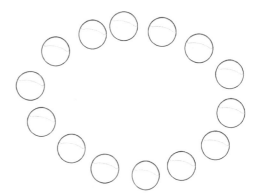

3. 3 + 4 + 4 = _____

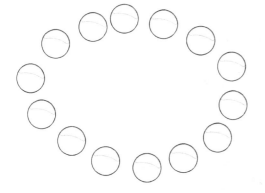

6. 2 + 3 + 5 = _____

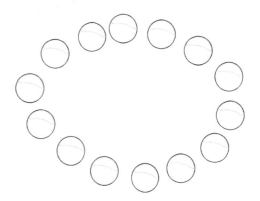

Use the number line to add three addends. Write the number sentence.

7.

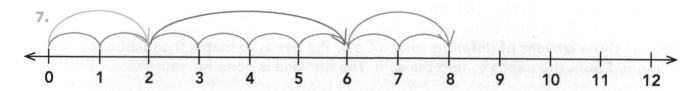

_____ + _____ + _____ = _____

8.

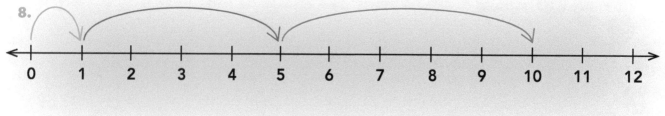

_____ + _____ + _____ = _____

Draw the hops for the addends on the number line. Write the sum.

9.

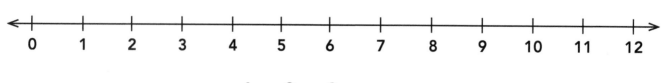

$4 + 2 + 3 =$ _____

10.

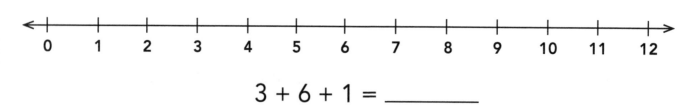

$3 + 6 + 1 =$ _____

Use connecting cubes to make a model of each number sentence. Add. Write the sum.

11. 🐢🐢 + 6 + 🐬 = _____

12. 7 + 🦈🦈 + 🐠 = _____

Add.

1.

$1 + 1 =$ _____

3.

$2 + 2 =$ _____

5.

$3 + 3 =$ _____

2.

$4 + 4 =$ _____

4.

$5 + 5 =$ _____

Find the pattern. Finish the sequence.

6. | 2   4   6   _____   _____   _____   _____   _____

7. | 18 16 _____   12 _____   _____   _____

Find the double. Count on one more.

8.  $2 + 3$

Use what you know: $2 + 2 = 4$

$2 + 3$ is one more: $2 + 3 =$ _____

9.  $3 + 4$

Use what you know: $3 + 3 = 6$

$3 + 4$ is one more: $3 + 4 =$ _____

10.  $5 + 6$

Use what you know: $5 + 5 = 10$

$5 + 6$ is one more: $5 + 6 =$ _____

Add.

11.
$$\begin{array}{r} 1 \\ +\ 2 \\ \hline \end{array}$$

12.
$$\begin{array}{r} 4 \\ +\ 5 \\ \hline \end{array}$$

13.
$$\begin{array}{r} 2 \\ +\ 3 \\ \hline \end{array}$$

14.
$$\begin{array}{r} 3 \\ +\ 4 \\ \hline \end{array}$$

Match. Complete the addition problems.

15.  •
    • $\begin{array}{r} 5 \\ +\ 1 \\ \hline \end{array}$

16.  •
    • $\begin{array}{r} 6 \\ +\ 5 \\ \hline \end{array}$

17.  •
    • $\begin{array}{r} 2 \\ +\ 4 \\ \hline \end{array}$

18.  •
    • $\begin{array}{r} 4 \\ +\ 4 \\ \hline \end{array}$

19. **Look at the picture. Circle the correct number sentence.**

$8 - 3 = 5$

$9 - 5 = 4$

$7 + 2 = 9$

Name _____

Tally the number shown by the number word. Use the tallies to make a number sentence. The first one is done for you.

number	tally marks	number sentence
1. eight	卌 |||	5 + 3 = 8
2. ten		☐ ☐ = 10
3. nine		☐ ☐ = 9
4. seven		☐ ☐ = 7

Add or subtract. Are the sums or differences in each row even or odd? Circle one.

5. 0 + 3 = ☐   6 − 1 = ☐   5 + 2 = ☐   even / odd

6. 11 − 9 = ☐   8 − 4 = ☐   6 + 0 = ☐   even / odd

Circle the one that is greater.

7. 8   2   9. 18   23   11. 35   27   13. 12   21

8. 7   5   10. 20   10   12. 9   12   14. 41   37

Solve. Circle the sum or difference in each pair that is less.

15. $4 + 5 =$ ____

16. $4 - 1 =$ ____

17. $9 - 5 =$ ____

$8 + 0 =$ ____

$6 - 2 =$ ____

$7 - 2 =$ ____

Solve. Circle the sum or difference in each pair that is greater.

18.
$$\begin{array}{r} 7 \\ -\ 5 \\ \hline \end{array} \qquad \begin{array}{r} 10 \\ -\ 2 \\ \hline \end{array}$$

19.
$$\begin{array}{r} 8 \\ -\ 6 \\ \hline \end{array} \qquad \begin{array}{r} 10 \\ -\ 5 \\ \hline \end{array}$$

20.
$$\begin{array}{r} 5 \\ +\ 3 \\ \hline \end{array} \qquad \begin{array}{r} 7 \\ +\ 2 \\ \hline \end{array}$$

Look at the picture. Write the answers.

21. How many ? _____

22. How many ? ____

23. How many ? ____

24. Add all the sea animals.

____ + ____ + ____ = ____

25. Add.

 $\square$

$+$  $\square$

$\square$

26. Subtract.

 $\square$

$-$ $\square$

$\square$

Name _____

Add to each set to make the number. Circle the set of triangles.

1.

2. 2

3. 9

Mark off extras to make a set of the number.

4. 5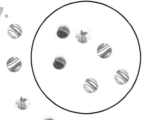

5. 10

6. 8

Write addition problems.

7.

outside ☐

+ inside ☐

——————

☐

8.

outside ☐

+ inside ☐

——————

☐

Write the fact families.

9.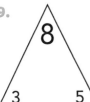

8

3   5

___ + ___ = ___

___ + ___ = ___

___ − ___ = ___

___ − ___ = ___

10.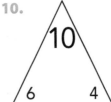

10

6   4

___ + ___ = ___

___ + ___ = ___

___ − ___ = ___

___ − ___ = ___

Add or subtract.

11.
$$\begin{array}{r} 4 \\ + 2 \\ \hline \end{array}$$

13.
$$\begin{array}{r} 6 \\ - 1 \\ \hline \end{array}$$

15.
$$\begin{array}{r} 8 \\ + 4 \\ \hline \end{array}$$

17.
$$\begin{array}{r} 10 \\ + 0 \\ \hline \end{array}$$

19.
$$\begin{array}{r} 9 \\ - 5 \\ \hline \end{array}$$

21.
$$\begin{array}{r} 7 \\ - 4 \\ \hline \end{array}$$

12.
$$\begin{array}{r} 10 \\ - 6 \\ \hline \end{array}$$

14.
$$\begin{array}{r} 8 \\ + 1 \\ \hline \end{array}$$

16.
$$\begin{array}{r} 5 \\ + 5 \\ \hline \end{array}$$

18.
$$\begin{array}{r} 11 \\ - 5 \\ \hline \end{array}$$

20.
$$\begin{array}{r} 6 \\ + 4 \\ \hline \end{array}$$

22.
$$\begin{array}{r} 11 \\ - 6 \\ \hline \end{array}$$

Count the money in each bank. Circle the bank with the least amount of money.

23.   24.   25.

26. **Circle the pictures that show shape reflection.**

Chapter 4
Time and Money

You care for the land and water it;
You enrich it abundantly.
The streams of God are filled with water
to provide the people with grain,
for so You have ordained it.
Psalm 65:9

Key Ideas:

Time: nearest hour, half hour, and quarter hour

Time: analog and digital clocks

Money: counting pennies, nickels, dimes, and quarters

Money: comparing amounts and solving word problems

10:00
ten o'clock

Draw a line from each clock to the time.

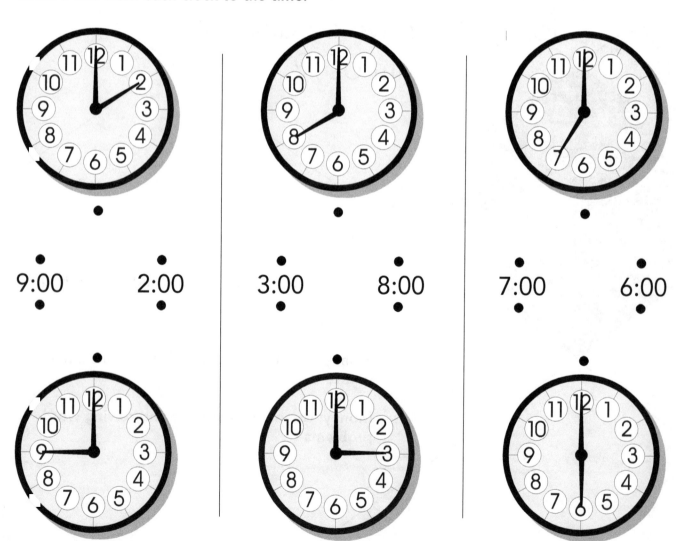

9:00   2:00   3:00   8:00   7:00   6:00

1. Draw a picture to represent each month of the year.

January	February	March	April
May	June	July	August
September	October	November	December

Answer the questions.

2. What is the first month of the school year?

_____

3. In what month is Jesus' birthday celebrated?

_____

4. In what month is your birthday?

_____

5. Fill in the name and dates for this month. Color the names of the school days blue.

Sunday	Monday	Tuesday	Wednesday	Thursday	Friday	Saturday

6. There are 7 days in a week. How many days are in 2 weeks?

_____ days

7. Circle today's date. How many days until the end of the month?

_____ days

There are 24 hours every day.

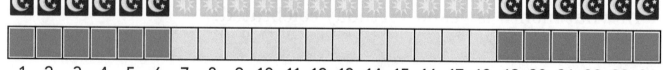

1 2 3 4 5 6 7 8 9 10 11 12 13 14 15 16 17 18 19 20 21 22 23 24

8. What time do you start school each day? _____ : _____

9. What time does your school day end? _____ : _____

→ The hour hand is shorter and tells the hour.

→ The minute hand is longer and tells the minutes.

1. Write the numerals. Circle the hour hand in red. Circle the minute hand in green.

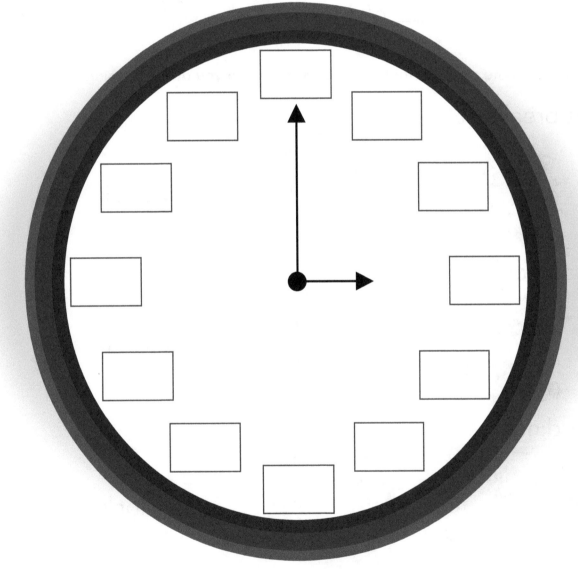

2. Color the arrow that goes clockwise.

Look at the hour hand. Write the time.

3.

_____ o'clock

4.

_____ o'clock

Draw hands on the clock. Write the times of day when you do these things.

5. eat breakfast

_____ o'clock

6. eat lunch

_____ o'clock

7. eat dinner

_____ o'clock

8. go to bed

_____ o'clock

Look at the two clocks. Is the time the same?

Cut out the rectangles with the digital times. Glue them under the standard clock or watch with the same time.

1.

3.

5.

2.

4.

6.

Draw the hands to show the time. For the half hour, be sure the hour hand is correct.

7.

5:00

8.
3:30

9.

8:00

Write the time.

10.

11.

12.

_____ : _____   _____ : _____   _____ : _____

Write the time.

13.
nine thirty

14.
four thirty
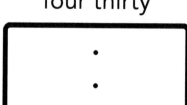

15.
two o'clock
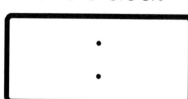

Name _____

Write the time.

1.

five o'clock

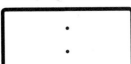

3.

five thirty

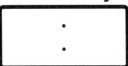

2.

five fifteen

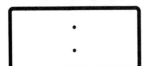

4.

five forty-five

Place these times in order starting with 12:00.

5.

| 2:15 |
| 4:30 |
| 12:00 |
| 3:45 |
| 9:00 |

Draw the minute hand.

6.

5:15

7.

7:45

8.

1:15

Draw the hour hand.

9.

2:30

10.

4:30

11.

3:45

12. Football practice started at 6:30.

Dave was 30 minutes late. What time did he arrive?

_____ : _____

Draw the time on the clock.

13. A trip across the lake takes 15 minutes. Lee's boat started at
7:15. What time did she land?

_____ : _____

Draw the time on the clock.

1. Write the minutes around the clock.

_____ 0 _____   _____ 5 _____

How many minutes are in the shaded area?

2.

3.

4.

_____ minutes   _____ minutes   _____ minutes

Show the minute hand on each clock

5. The boat race started at 9:00.

6. The winner crossed the finish line 45 minutes later.

Write the time.

7.

8.

9.

Write the time.

Draw the hands on the clock.

17. Cut out the pictures. Glue them under the time of day that you do those activities. Write the time.

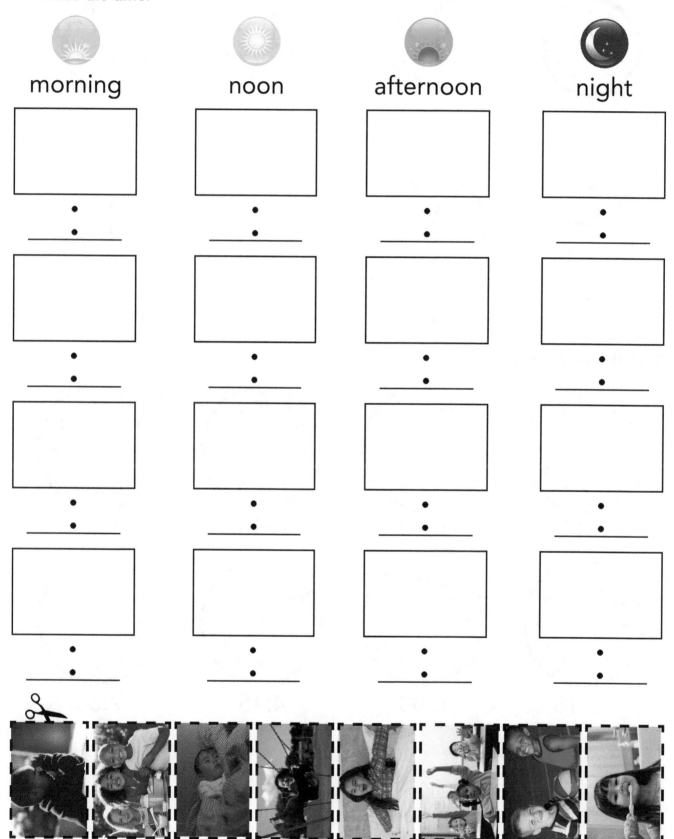

morning   noon   afternoon   night

Name _____

1. Match the digital times to the right clock.

●   ●   ●   ●

●   ●   ●   ●

| 8:00 | 10:30 | 1:30 | 5:15 |

2. It takes 30 minutes to bake a cake. If you put the cake in the oven at 2:30, when will you take it out?

_____ : _____

3. The baby turtle hatched at midnight, 12:00. It took 2 hours to reach the sea. What time did it get there?

_____ : _____

4. Circle candle that would take longer to burn.

5. Circle the ice cream cone that would take longer to eat.

The cars started the race at  . The flags show when they finished the race.

What place did each car earn? Write the place.

Word Bank
1st   2nd   3rd   4th   5th   6th

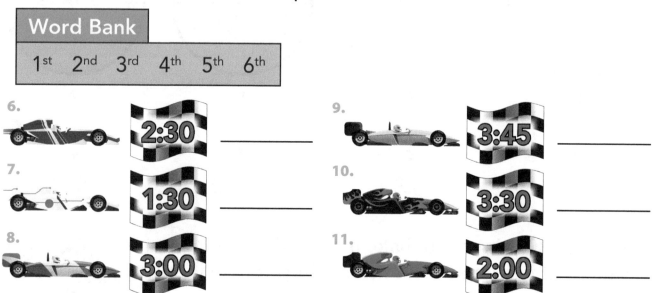

6. 2:30 _____

7. 1:30 _____

8. 3:00 _____

9. 3:45 _____

10. 3:30 _____

11. 2:00 _____

Look at the first clock. On the second clock, draw the hands that show the time ...

12. in 15 minutes.

4:00

13. in 60 minutes.

9:30

14. in 3 hours.

6:15

Pennies, Nickels, and Dimes 4.8

1. Write the words five, ten, and one to complete the sentences.

A penny is _____ cent. Count pennies by 1s.

A nickel is _____ cents. Count nickels by 5s.

A dime is _____ cents. Count dimes by 10s.

Count the coins in each row. Write the total amount of money.

2.    = _____ ¢

3.    = _____ ¢

4.   = _____ ¢

5.   = _____ ¢

Write the amount.

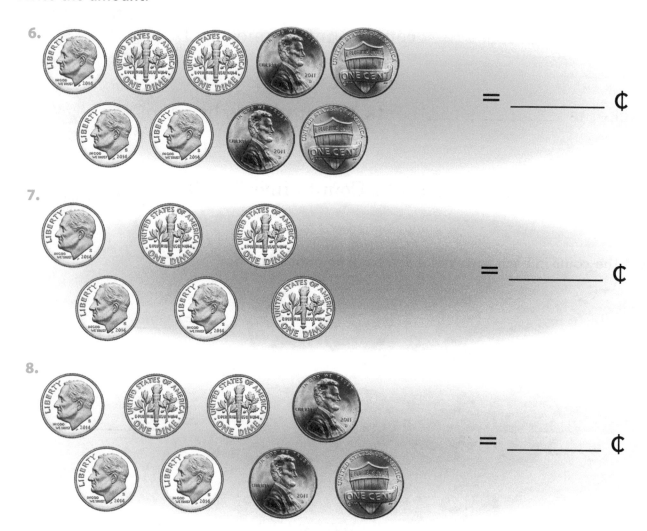

6. = _____ ¢

7. = _____ ¢

8. = _____ ¢

Match.

9. • • 23¢

10. • • 42¢

11. • • 17¢

Use the hundred chart to help you count on.

1	2	3	4	5	6	7	8	9	**10**
11	12	13	14	15	16	17	18	19	**20**
21	22	23	24	25	26	27	28	29	**30**
31	32	33	34	35	36	37	38	39	**40**
41	42	43	44	45	46	47	48	49	50
51	52	53	54	55	56	57	58	59	60
61	62	63	64	65	66	67	68	69	70
71	72	73	74	75	76	77	78	79	80
81	82	83	84	85	86	87	88	89	90
91	92	93	94	95	96	97	98	99	100

Keep a running count. Write the amount. The first one is done for you.

1.

_10_ _20_ _30_ _40_ _45_ = _45_ ¢

2.

____ ____ ____ ____ ____ = ____ ¢

3.

____ ____ ____ ____ ____ = ____ ¢

Keep a running count. Write the amount.

4.

_____ _____ _____ _____ _____ _____ = _____ ¢

5.

_____ _____ _____ _____ _____ _____ = _____ ¢

6.

_____ _____ _____ _____ _____ _____ = _____ ¢

7. **Count the coins. Circle the money needed to buy 1 fish.**

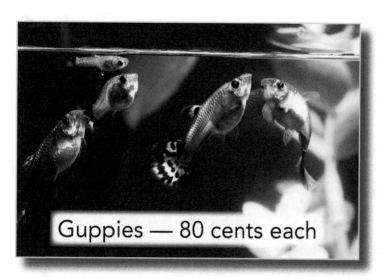

Guppies — 80 cents each

Compare Sets of Coins **4.10**

Count the coins in each exercise.

Compare the amounts. Which is greater? Fill in the circle.

1.

○

○

3.

○

○

2.

○

○

4.

○

○

Which is less? Fill in the circle.

5.

○

○

6.

○

○

Count the coins. Compare the amount to the price of each fish. Do you have enough to buy the fish? Circle yes or no.

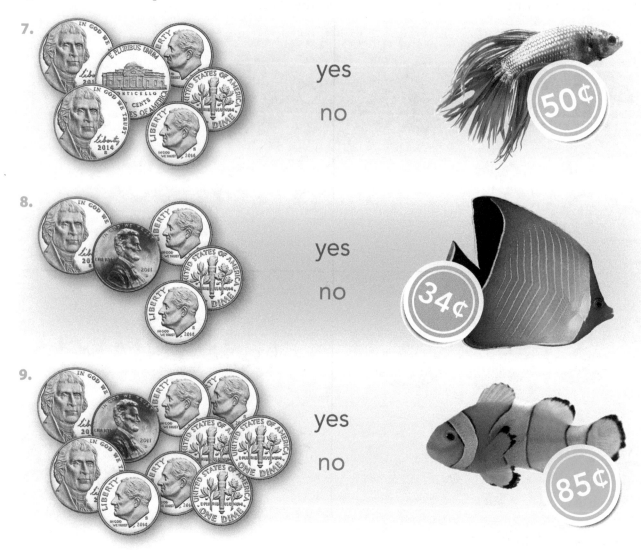

7. yes

   no

8. yes

   no

9. yes

   no

Review

Write the time.

10.

11.

12.

Count Coins to One Dollar 4.11

100¢ or $1.00

20 nickels

4 quarters

10 dimes

100 pennies

A dollar is 100 cents. One dollar is equal to 100 pennies, 10 dimes, 20 nickels, or 4 quarters. A quarter is 25 cents.

Keep a running count. Write the amount.

1.

_____ _____ _____ = _____ ¢ or $_____

2.

_____ _____ = _____ ¢

3.

_____ _____ _____ = _____ ¢

Circle the coins needed to make $1.00. You will not need all the coins.

4.

5.

6.

Look at the prices of the fish for sale at the pet shop.

Circle the coins needed to buy each fish.

1.

2.

Solve.

3. Kim has 1 . She has 1 . She has 2 .

Which fish can she buy? Circle it.

Circle the amount needed.

4. How much are 3  ?   10¢   15¢

5. How much are 2 ?   20¢   25¢

6. How much are 1 and 1 ?   10¢   15¢

7. How much are 2 ?   30¢   50¢

Solve. Circle yes or no.

8. Zack has 1 . Can he buy 2 ?   yes   no

9. Can Zack buy 3 ?   yes   no

10. Can Zack buy 1 ?   yes   no

Coins: Add and Subtract 4.13

 2¢

 4¢

6¢

3¢

How much money do you need? Write the problems. Solve.

1.
+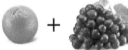

	2¢
+	4¢
	¢

2.
+

	¢
+	¢
	¢

3.
+

	¢
+	¢
	¢

4. + + ___ ¢ + ___ ¢ + ___ ¢ = _____ ¢

5. ___ ¢ + ___ ¢ + ___ ¢ = _____ ¢

How much change will you get?

6. 10
−

10¢
− 2¢
¢

7. 10
−

¢
− ¢
¢

8. 10
−

¢
− ¢
¢

Add.

9.   6¢
  + 1¢
  ___
    ¢

10.   9¢
  + 0¢
  ___
    ¢

11.   4¢
  + 5¢
  ___
    ¢

12.   1¢
  + 1¢
  ___
    ¢

13.   7¢
  + 3¢
  ___
    ¢

Subtract.

14.   5¢
  − 2¢
  ___
    ¢

15.   7¢
  − 3¢
  ___
    ¢

16.   4¢
  − 1¢
  ___
    ¢

17.   8¢
  − 7¢
  ___
    ¢

18.   10¢
  − 5¢
  ___
    ¢

Solve.

19. Tomás had 11¢. He lost 6¢. How much is left?

Mark off to subtract. Write a number sentence.

_____ ¢ − _____ ¢ = _____ ¢

20. Kelly had 9¢. She found 2¢. How much does she have in all?

Circle the coins Kelly had in red. Circle the coins she found in blue.

Write a number sentence.

_____ ¢ + _____ ¢ = _____ ¢

Write the time.

1.

· ·

2.

· ·

3.

· ·

4.

· ·

5.

· ·

6.

· ·

7.

· ·

8.

· ·

Write the amount.

9.  = _____ ¢

10.  = _____ ¢

11.  = _____ ¢

Solve.

12. Sanjay's party begins at 3:00. It will last two hours. What time will the party end?

_____ : _____

13. Bella rides her bike for one hour. She begins at 12:00. What time does she stop riding?

_____ : _____

14. Aya has five cents. She finds a dime on the sidewalk. How much money does she have now?

_____ ¢

15. Len has 15 cents. He spends 10 cents. How much money does Len have left?

_____ ¢

16. Juma has 2 dimes. How much money does Juma have?

_____ ¢

Juma's brother has 3 nickels and 3 pennies.
Does Juma have more money than his brother?

yes   no

Chapter 5
Place Value

Therefore God exalted Him to the highest place and gave Him the name that is above every name, that at the name of Jesus every knee should bow...
Philippians 2:9–10a

Key Ideas:

Place Value: tens and ones, whole numbers to hundreds, using place value to add and subtract

Addition: adding two-digit numbers

Subtraction: subtracting two-digit numbers

Circle sets of 10 fish.

I circled ＿＿＿＿＿＿ sets of 10. ＿＿＿＿＿＿ fish are left.

Make sets of 10.

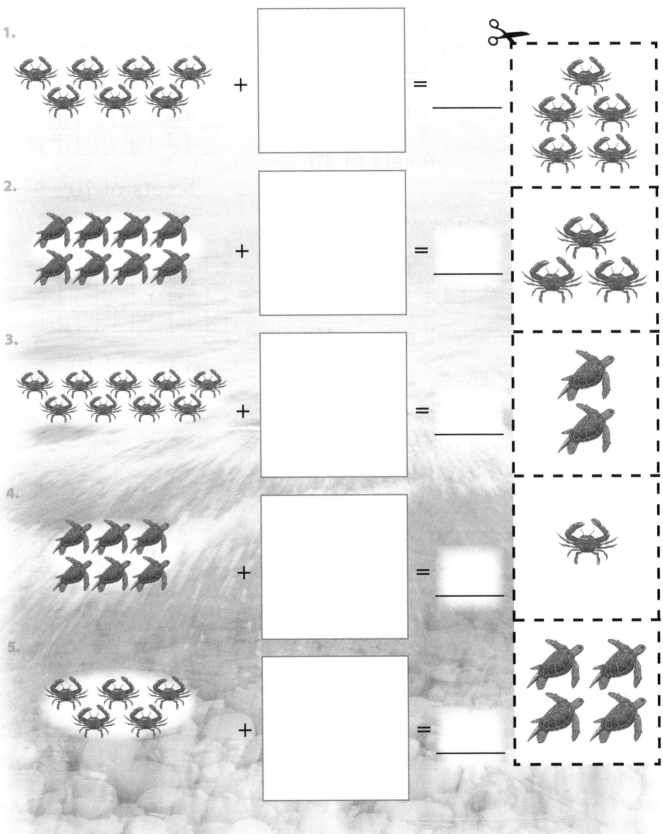

1. _____ + [ ] = _____

2. _____ + [ ] = _____

3. _____ + [ ] = _____

4. _____ + [ ] = _____

5. _____ + [ ] = _____

Circle the greater number.

6.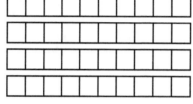

4 sets of 10

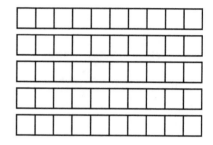

5 sets of 10

Circle the number that is less.

7.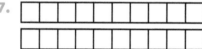

2 sets of 10

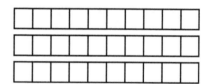

3 sets of 10

Review

Add. Look for patterns in the sums.

8.
$$\begin{array}{r} 5 \\ + 2 \end{array} \quad \begin{array}{r} 5 \\ + 3 \end{array} \quad \begin{array}{r} 5 \\ + 4 \end{array}$$

10.
$$\begin{array}{r} 4 \\ + 4 \end{array} \quad \begin{array}{r} 4 \\ + 3 \end{array} \quad \begin{array}{r} 4 \\ + 2 \end{array}$$

9.
$$\begin{array}{r} 3 \\ + 3 \end{array} \quad \begin{array}{r} 4 \\ + 4 \end{array} \quad \begin{array}{r} 5 \\ + 5 \end{array}$$

11.
$$\begin{array}{r} 4 \\ + 3 \end{array} \quad \begin{array}{r} 6 \\ + 1 \end{array} \quad \begin{array}{r} 7 \\ + 0 \end{array}$$

Circle sets of 10. Write the number of tens.

1.

|||| |||| |||| |||| ||||
|||| |||| ||||

3.

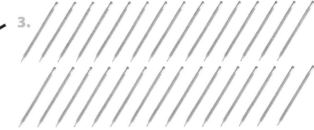

_____ tens = _____

_____ tens = _____

2.

4.

_____ tens = _____

_____ tens = _____

Color each set of 10 a different color.

5.

6.

7.

Cut out the tens and ones squares at the bottom of the page. Glue them to match.

8.	10.
2 tens 3 ones	3 tens 2 ones
9.	11.
4 tens 5 ones	5 tens 4 ones

Review

12. **Write the time.**

:

Show one hour earlier. Write the time.

:

Add.

13.	14.	15.	16.	17.	18.
4 + 5	5 + 3	7 + 4	9 + 3	3 + 4	6 + 4

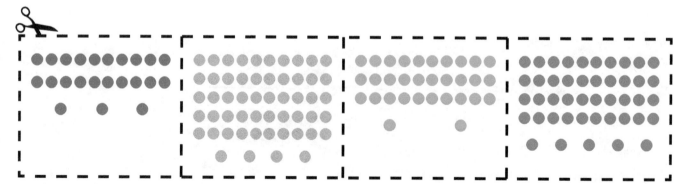

Two-Digit Numerals 5.3

A digit is any one of the numerals from 0 to 9. Place value is the value of a digit depending on its place in a number. Five tens are 50. Five ones are only 5.

Write the tens and ones. Write the total.

1.

_____ tens _____ ones = _____

2.
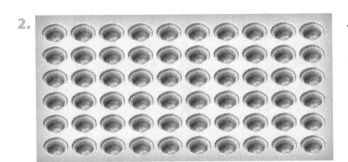

_____ tens _____ ones = _____

3.

_____ tens _____ ones = _____

4.

_____ tens _____ ones = _____

5.

_____ tens _____ ones = _____

6.
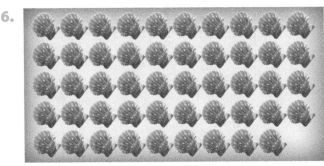

_____ tens _____ ones = _____

7.

_____ tens _____ ones = _____

Write the tens and ones.

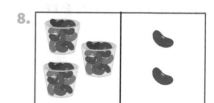

8. | | | 9. | | | 10. | | |

_____ tens _____ ones _____ tens _____ ones _____ tens _____ ones

Use the ten-frames to write the tens and ones.

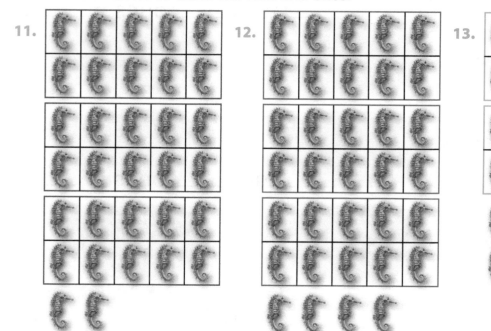

11. 12. 13.

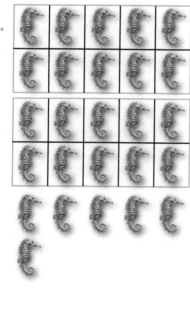

_____ tens _____ ones | _____ tens _____ ones | _____ tens _____ ones

Write the tens and ones. Write the total.

14.

_____ tens _____ ones = _____ ¢

15.

_____ tens _____ ones = _____ ¢

Name _____

Write the number of tens and ones on each place value mat. Write the total. Circle the larger number in each pair.

1.

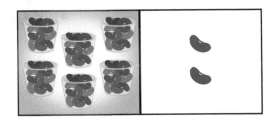

_____ tens _____ ones = _____   _____ tens _____ ones = _____

2.

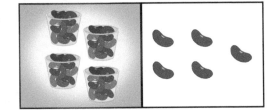

_____ tens _____ ones = _____   _____ tens _____ ones = _____

Count. Write the number of tens and ones. Write the total.

3.

_____ tens _____ ones = _____

4.

_____ tens _____ ones = _____

5. Draw bundles of tens to show 30 straws.

Match the picture with the correct number.

6.    •

7.   •

8.   •

• 40

• 4

• 50

9.   •

10.   •

11.   •

12.   •

• 6

• 5

• 60

• 20

Review

Count. Write the tens and ones. Then, write the total.

13. 

_____ tens _____ ones = _____

15.  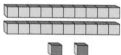

_____ tens _____ ones = _____

14.

_____ tens _____ ones = _____

16.

_____ tens _____ ones = _____

Name _____

Match.

1.

2.

3.

4.

Count the tens and ones. Fill in the correct circle.

5.   ○ 59   ○ 95

6. 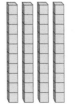   ○ 54   ○ 45

7.   ○ 34   ○ 43

Count. Write the numerals.

8.

_____ tens _____ ones

= _____

9.

_____ tens _____ ones

= _____

10.

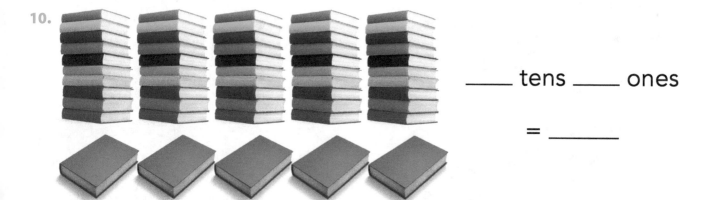

_____ tens _____ ones

= _____

11.

_____ tens _____ ones

= _____

Write the amount.

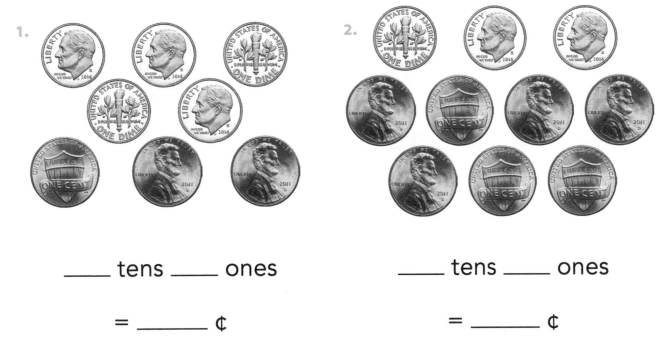

1.

2.

____ tens ____ ones

____ tens ____ ones

= _____ ¢

= _____ ¢

3. José, Ana, and Leah collected dimes and pennies for their church. The graph shows how many of each kind of coin they collected.

Read the graph. Write the total.

Coin Graph

name	number of coins
José	
Ana	
Leah	

José ____ ¢   Ana ____ ¢   Leah ____ ¢

Write the amount.

4.

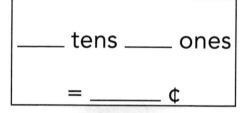

_____ tens _____ ones

= _____ ¢

5.

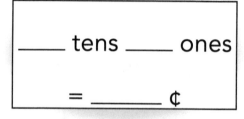

_____ tens _____ ones

= _____ ¢

6.

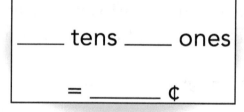

_____ tens _____ ones

= _____ ¢

Circle the set of coins that each child has.

7. Sara has 52¢.

8. Ross has 25¢.

Count the amounts and write the problem. Add.

1.

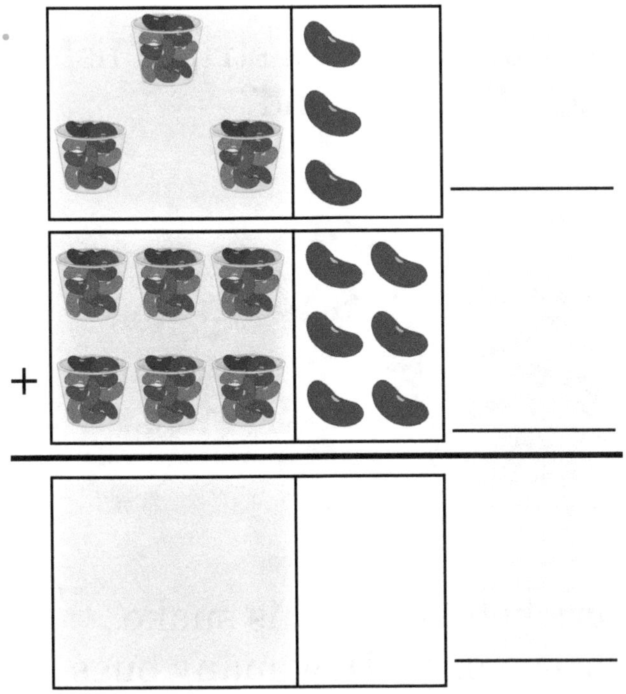

_____

+

_____

_____

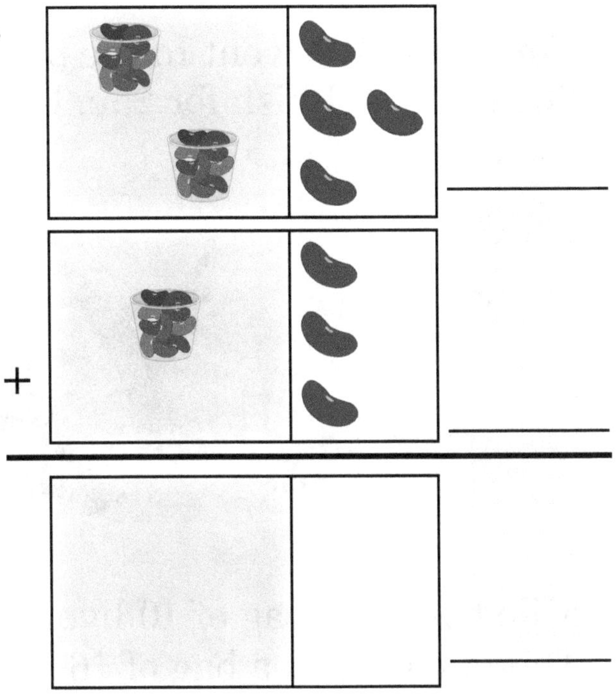

2.

_____

+

_____

_____

3.

_____

+

_____

_____

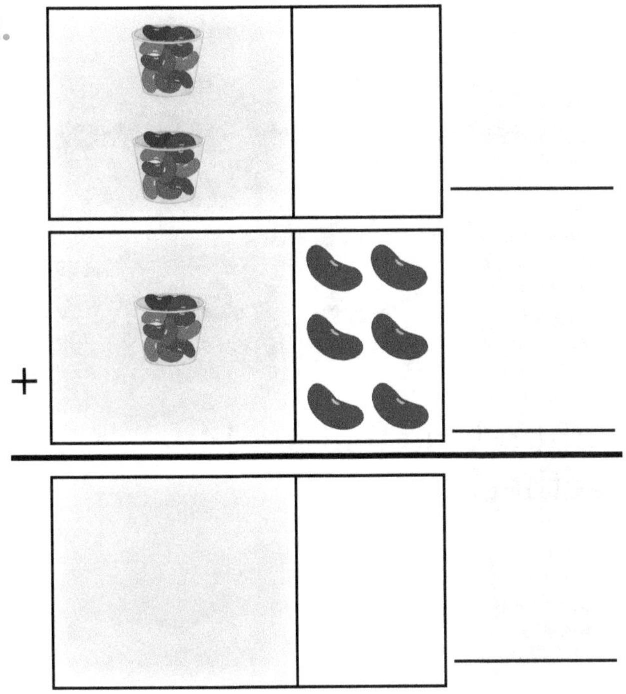

4.

_____

+

_____

_____

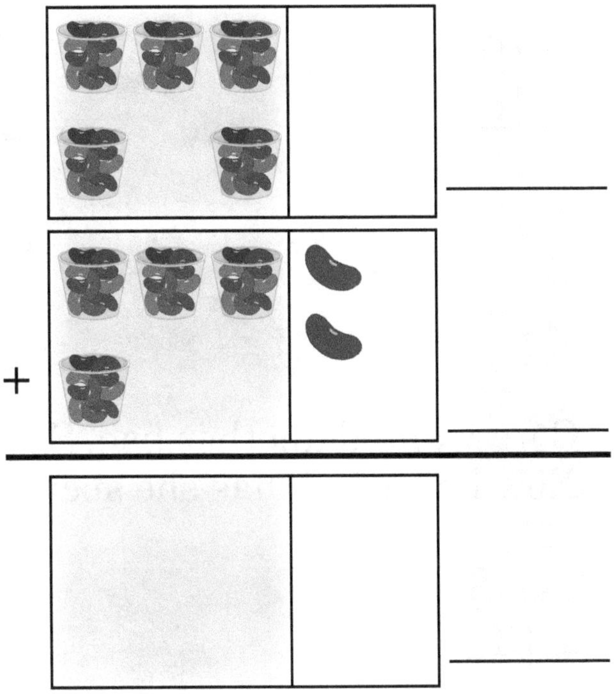

Read and think. Write the numbers. Solve.

5. Cora and Milo went to the pet store. Cora bought a striped fish for 50¢ and a goldfish for 25¢. How much did she spend?

$$\begin{array}{r} 50¢ \\ +25¢ \\ \hline ¢ \end{array}$$

6. Milo bought a bag of 10 live black crickets to feed his snake. Then he bought a bag of 16 dried brown ones. How many bugs did he buy?

$$\begin{array}{r} 10 \\ +16 \\ \hline \end{array}$$

7. Cora wanted another fish. She bought a blue fish for 14¢. Now how much has she spent altogether?

$$\begin{array}{r} ¢ \\ +14¢ \\ \hline ¢ \end{array}$$

Name _____

Write the answer to each exercise.

1.

tens	ones
2	5
− 1	4

2.

2 tens 5 ones
− 1 ten   4 ones
_____

3.

25
− 14
_____

Subtract.

4.

tens	ones
6	1
− 4	0

5.

tens	ones
7	4
− 3	1

6.

tens	ones
5	8
− 4	6

7.

44
− 22
_____

8.

28
− 17
_____

9.

73
− 41
_____

Subtract.

10.
$$90 - 20 = \boxed{}$$

12.
$$80 - 60 = \boxed{}$$

14.
$$40 - 10 = \boxed{}$$

16.
$$50 - 40 = \boxed{}$$

11.
$$30 - 30 = \boxed{}$$

13.
$$70 - 50 = \boxed{}$$

15.
$$60 - 30 = \boxed{}$$

17.
$$20 - 10 = \boxed{}$$

Read and think. Write the numbers. Solve.

18. Jack collected 26 shells at the beach. Lee collected 38 shells. How many more did Lee collect than Jack?

$$38 - 26 = \boxed{} \text{ shells}$$

19. Nan bought 39 sand dollars. Sue bought 17 starfish. How many more did Nan buy than Sue?

$$39 - 17 = \boxed{}$$

Choose + or –.

1.   18
     9
     9

3.   36
     12
     48

5.   45
     44
     89

7.   22
     7
     29

2.   73
     21
     94

4.   99
     0
     99

6.   51
     30
     21

8.   29
     19
     10

Does the answer make sense? Circle yes or no.

9.   yes   no
     27
   + 12
     25

10. yes   no
     19
   – 12
     7

11. yes   no
     46
   + 23
     48

12. yes   no
     51
   + 11
     40

Match.

13.   4 tens 0 ones •   • 43

14.   40 and 3 •   • 41

15.   41 + 0 •   • 40

Solve.

16.
$$\begin{array}{r} 14 \\ + 21 \\ \hline \end{array}$$

18.
$$\begin{array}{r} 19 \\ - 7 \\ \hline \end{array}$$

20.
$$\begin{array}{r} 91 \\ - 80 \\ \hline \end{array}$$

22.
$$\begin{array}{r} 36 \\ - 15 \\ \hline \end{array}$$

17.
$$\begin{array}{r} 22 \\ + 33 \\ \hline \end{array}$$

19.
$$\begin{array}{r} 78 \\ - 38 \\ \hline \end{array}$$

21.
$$\begin{array}{r} 64 \\ - 52 \\ \hline \end{array}$$

23.
$$\begin{array}{r} 49 \\ - 27 \\ \hline \end{array}$$

Match.

24.
$$\begin{array}{r} 45 \\ + 54 \\ \hline \end{array}$$ •   • 54

25.
$$\begin{array}{r} 54 \\ - 23 \\ \hline \end{array}$$ •   • 31

26.
$$\begin{array}{r} 99 \\ - 54 \\ \hline \end{array}$$ •   • 99

27.
$$\begin{array}{r} 99 \\ - 45 \\ \hline \end{array}$$ •   • 45

Name _____

Read and think. Write the numbers. Write + or −. Solve.

1. Raj counted 25 gulls. Then 14 gulls flew away.
   How many are left?

_____ gulls

tens	ones

2. Sam saw 24 shells on the sand. Ava saw
   53 shells. How many did they see in all?

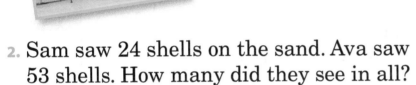
_____ shells

tens	ones

3. Brent walked on the beach for 22 minutes.
   He swam for 35 minutes. How much time
   did he spend walking and swimming?

_____ minutes

tens	ones

Read and think. Write the numbers. Write + or −. Solve.

4. Max saw 49 baby turtles. 25 went into the water. How many were still on the sand?

_____ turtles

tens	ones

5. Beth saw 20 kites one morning. She saw 16 kites in the afternoon. How many kites did she see altogether?

_____ kites

tens	ones

6. Lupita found 23 starfish on the beach. She is putting them in the water. So far she has put 11 back in. How many are left to go?

_____ starfish

tens	ones

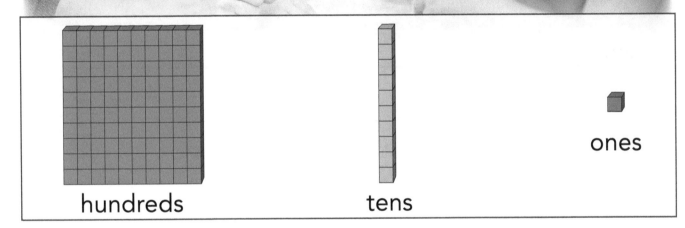

hundreds   tens   ones

Read the words. Write the numbers.

1. two hundred fifty-three   _____

2. six hundred sixty-seven   _____

3. four hundred twenty   _____

4. one hundred thirty-four   _____

5. seven hundred forty-nine   _____

6. three hundred seventy-two   _____

7. five hundred fifty   _____

Example: 243
                  two hundred forty-three
                  2 hundreds, 4 tens, and 3 ones

Word Bank

| twenty-nine | forty-six |
| seventy-four | hundred |

Write the number two ways.

8.

374 _____

_____

9.

129 _____

_____

10.

246 _____

_____

Name _____

1. Write O for ones, T for tens, and H for hundreds to tell the value of the underlined digit.

1 _8_ 9   4 6 _1_   _7_ 3 2

_____   _____   _____

Write the digit.

2. How many tens are in 952? _____

3. How many ones are in 246? _____

4. How many hundreds are in 380? _____

5. How many ones are in 729? _____

Write the number.

6. 2 sets of one hundred = _____

7. 6 sets of ten = _____

8. 4 ones = _____

9. 9 sets of ten = _____

10. 7 sets of one hundred = _____

Write each digit in the correct place. Write the number.

11.

hundreds	tens	ones

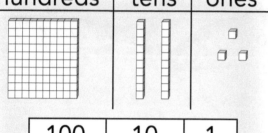

100	10	1

[   ]

12.

hundreds	tens	ones

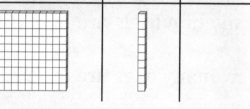

100	10	1

[   ]

13.

hundreds	tens	ones

100	10	1

[   ]

14.

hundreds	tens	ones

100	10	1

[   ]

Add.

15.

h	t	o
8	0	0
	5	0
+		9

16.

h	t	o
6	0	0
	1	0
+		7

17.

h	t	o
5	0	0
	9	0
+		5

Read and follow the clues. Trace the path to find the treasure.

1. Start at the number that has 1 ten and 5 ones.
2. Add ten.
3. Move ahead to the number that has 3 tens and 0 ones.
4. Go to the next even number.
5. Add ten.
6. Count on 8.
7. Add ten.
8. Go to the next number that has 5 ones.
9. Add ten.
10. Count on 5.
11. Add ten.
12. Go to the next number that has a 2 in the ones place.

13. The treasure is on number _____

Use your hundred chart to complete the puzzles.

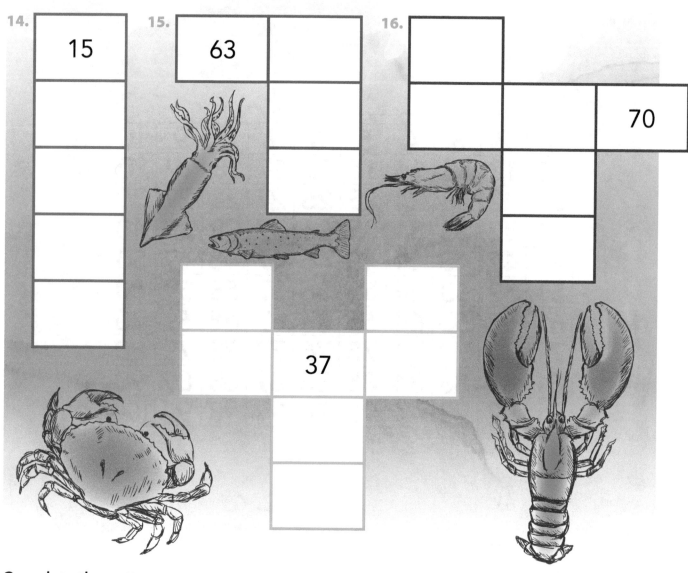

14. | 15 |

15. | 63 |

16. (with 70)

(center cross puzzle with 37)

Complete the patterns.

18. 25 ___ ___ 45 ___ ___ 75

19. 4 ___ 14 ___ ___ ___ ___

20. 11 ___ 13 ___ ___ ___ 21

Circle groups of 10. Write the number.

1.

2.

tens	ones

total

tens	ones

total

Count the tens and ones. Write the number.

3.

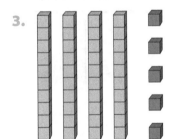

tens	ones

total

4.

tens	ones

total

Mark off to subtract.

5.

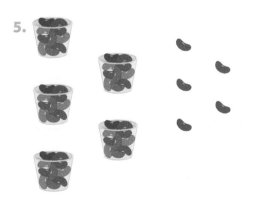

$$5 \text{ tens } 5 \text{ ones}$$
$$- 3 \text{ tens } 4 \text{ ones}$$

_____ tens _____ ones = _____

Add.

6.

tens	ones
2	1
+ 3	7

7.

tens	ones
7	2
+ 1	6

8.

tens	ones
6	4
+	5

Subtract.

9.

tens	ones
4	6
− 2	0

10.

tens	ones
5	3
− 4	3

11.

tens	ones
9	9
− 6	7

Write the digit.

12. How many tens are in 387? _____

13. How many ones are in 417? _____

14. How many hundreds are in 984? _____

Write the number.

15. $100 + 30 + 5 =$ _____

16. $700 + 40 + 6 =$ _____

17. $900 + 70 + 2 =$ _____

18. 2 groups of ten = _____

19. 3 groups of ten = _____

20. 4 ones = _____

Chapter 6
Measurement

Give, and it will be given to you. A good
measure, pressed down, shaken together and
running over, will be poured into your lap.
For with the measure you use, it will be
measured to you.
Luke 6:38

Key Ideas:

Measurement: nonstandard units

Measurement: customary and metric units of
length, capacity, and weight

Measurement: temperature

Geometry: three-dimensional figures: cones,
cubes, cylinders, spheres

1. Circle the longer fish.

2. Circle the container that holds more water.

Which is longer? Circle it.

1.

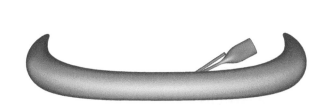

2.

Which is shorter? Circle it.

3.

4.
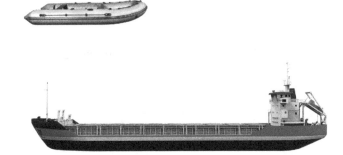

5. Put your crayon in the box. Put the end of the crayon at the left end of the box. Use your pencil to mark its length. Is your crayon longer or shorter than the crayon shown? Circle the longer crayon.

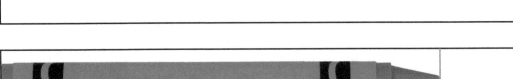

Use these real objects. Measure them with large paper clips.

6.

_____ paper clips

8.

_____ paper clips

7.

_____ paper clips

9.

_____ paper clips

Measure the objects with connecting cubes.

10.

_____ cubes

12.

_____ cubes

11.

_____ cubes

13.

_____ cubes

An inch is a unit of measurement in the customary system.

Compare your own objects with the ones below. Circle what is true. Then, place your object on the ruler. Write the length on the line.

longer than

1. My pencil is the same as the one here. It is about _____ inches.

shorter than

longer than

2. My crayon is the same as the one here. It is about _____ inches.

shorter than

longer than

3. My scissors are the same as the ones here. They are about _____ inches.

shorter than

longer than

4. My glue stick is the same as the one here. It is about _____ inches.

shorter than

Use an inch ruler. Measure these objects.

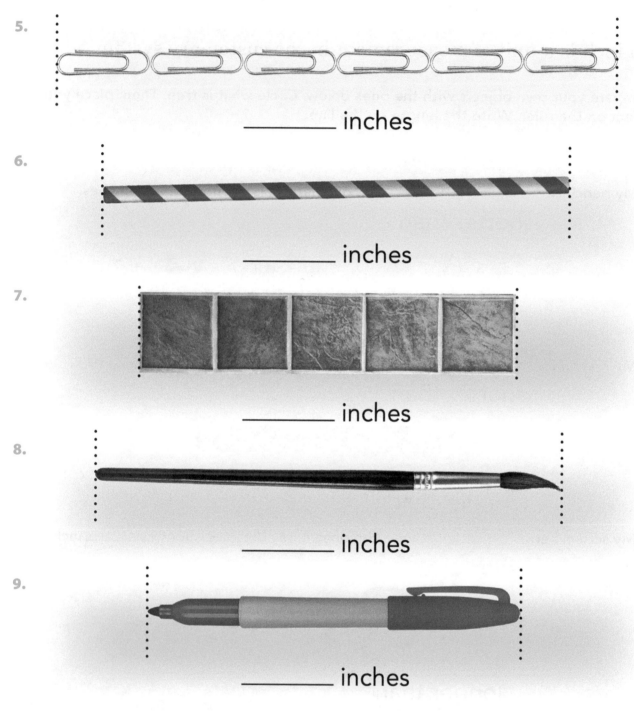

5. _____ inches

6. _____ inches

7. _____ inches

8. _____ inches

9. _____ inches

10. One pencil is 5 inches long. Another pencil is 4 inches long. How long would they be if you put them end-to-end? Write and solve the problem. Fill in the blank.

☐ ◯ ☐ = ☐ _____ inches

Name _____

A centimeter is a unit of measurement in the metric system.

Compare your own objects with the ones below. Circle what is true. Then, place your object on the ruler. Write the length on the line.

1. My pencil is
longer than
the same as
shorter than
the one here. It is about _____ centimeters.

2. My crayon is
longer than
the same as
shorter than
the one here. It is about _____ centimeters.

3. My scissors are
longer than
the same as
shorter than
the one here. They are about _____ centimeters.

4. My glue stick is
longer than
the same as
shorter than
the one here. It is about _____ centimeters.

Use a centimeter ruler. Measure these objects.

5.

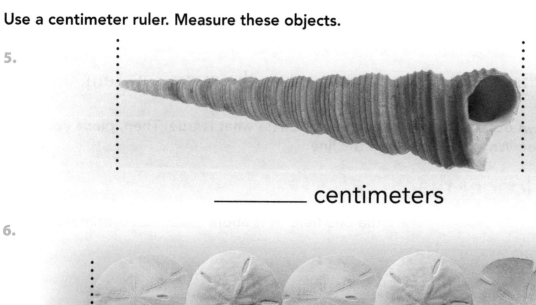

_____ centimeters

6.

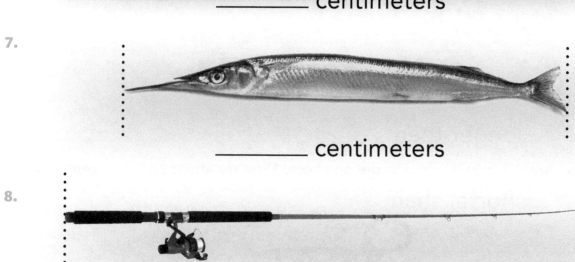

_____ centimeters

7.

_____ centimeters

8.

_____ centimeters

9.

_____ centimeters

1. Match.

3 inches •

5 centimeters •

2. Measure the fish. Circle the fish that is exactly 1 inch long.

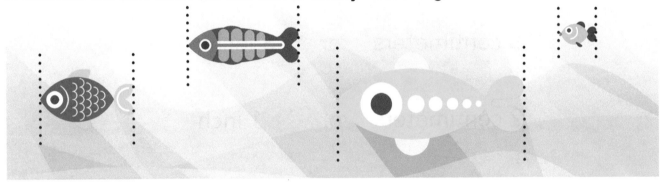

3. Measure the shells. Circle the shell that is exactly 2 centimeters long.

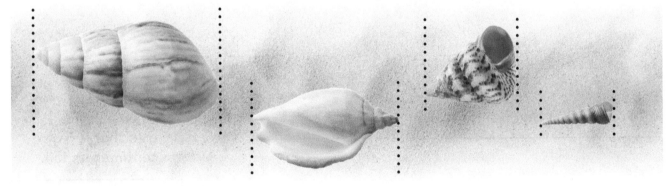

4. Circle the crab's trail that is exactly 3 inches long.

5. Which picture shows the correct way to measure a crayon? Circle it.

Circle the longer measurement.

6.

8 centimeters   or   3 inches

7.

2 centimeters   or   1 inch

8.

3 centimeters   or   3 inches

9.

13 centimeters   or   5 inches

10. Draw a boat that is 4 inches long.

11. Draw a palm tree that is 5 centimeters tall.

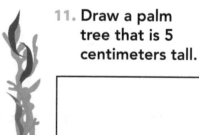

A foot is 12 inches. A yard is 36 inches. A yard is also 3 feet.

ruler

12 inches = 1 foot

yardstick

3 feet = 1 yard

1. **Would you use a ruler or a yardstick to measure each item? Circle your choice.**

ruler or yardstick

ruler or yardstick

ruler or yardstick

ruler or yardstick

2. Is the real object longer or shorter than 1 foot? Circle your answer.

longer or shorter

longer or shorter

longer or shorter

longer or shorter

longer or shorter

longer or shorter

3. Mia needs 2 yards of fabric for a Bible costume. How many feet does she need? Fill in the blank.

_____ feet

A meter is a metric unit of measurement. It equals 100 centimeters.

centimeter ruler

meterstick

Would you use a ruler or a meterstick to measure each animal? Circle your choice.

1.

ruler or meterstick

3.

ruler or meterstick

2.

ruler or meterstick

4.

ruler or meterstick

5. Which is the shortest unit? Fill in the circle.

◯ meter   ◯ yard   ◯ centimeter   ◯ inch   ◯ foot

6. Which is the longest unit? Fill in the circle.

◯ meter   ◯ yard   ◯ centimeter   ◯ inch   ◯ foot

Put an X on the word that does not belong in the set.

7.

yard

meter

foot

inch

customary units

8.

centimeter

meter

inch

metric units

9. Mrs. Chavez needs 200 centimeters of ribbon. Which tool should she use to measure the ribbon? Fill in the circle.

◯

◯

◯

◯

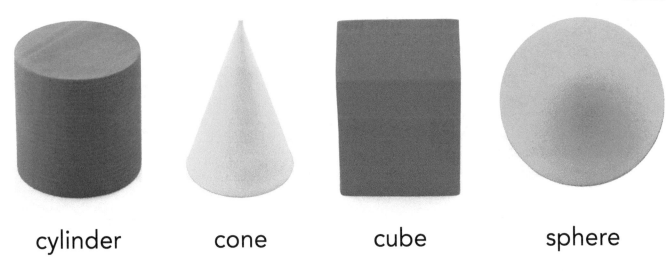

cylinder   cone   cube   sphere

1. Color the shapes. Use the colors in the box below.

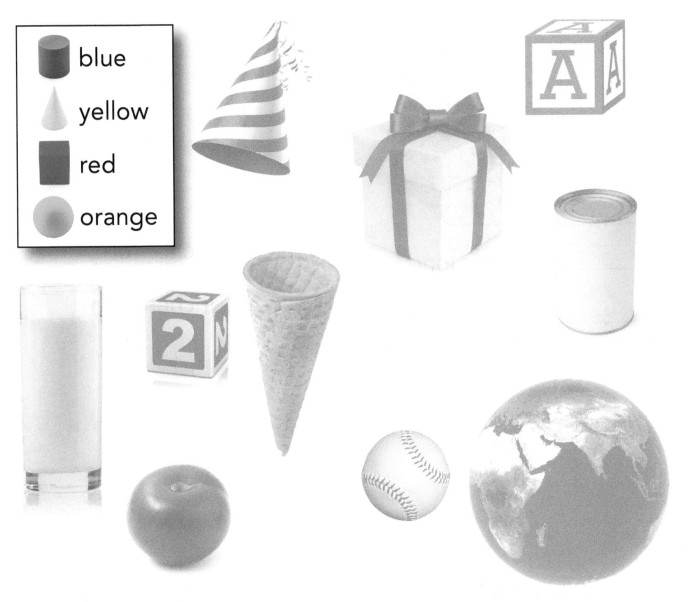

blue

yellow

red

orange

2. Measure each cylinder in inches. Write the length.

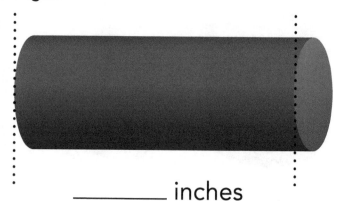

_____ inches

_____ inches

3. Measure each cube in inches. Write the length and height.

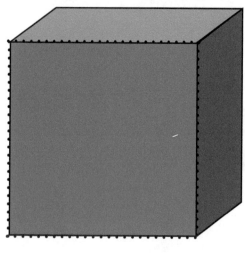

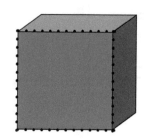

_____ inches long

_____ inches high

_____ inches long

_____ inches high

4. Measure the height of each box in centimeters.

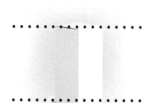

_____ centimeters

_____ centimeters

Circle the container that holds less.

1.

2.

Circle the container that holds more.

3.

5.

4.

6.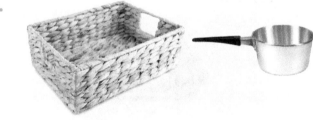

7. **Which container could hold the fish? Circle it.**

8. **Which container could hold the dog? Circle it.**

Circle your answer.

9. Mom needs to buy 25 boxes of cereal at the store. Which basket should she use?

10. Ten children are going on a picnic. Which cooler would hold their drinks and snacks?

11. Becca has 4 brothers. Which car would be the best fit for her and her family?

12. Put an X on the things that would not fit in the box.

Cups, Pints, Quarts, and Gallons 6.9

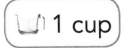 1 cup

  = 1 pint

= = 1 quart

= = 1 gallon

A cup is a customary unit used to measure capacity. A pint is equal to 2 cups. A quart is equal to 2 pints or 4 cups. A gallon is equal to 4 quarts, 8 pints, or 16 cups.

Draw each of the customary units in order from the smallest unit to the largest.

1.

3.

2.

4.

Make the amounts equal. The first one is done for you.

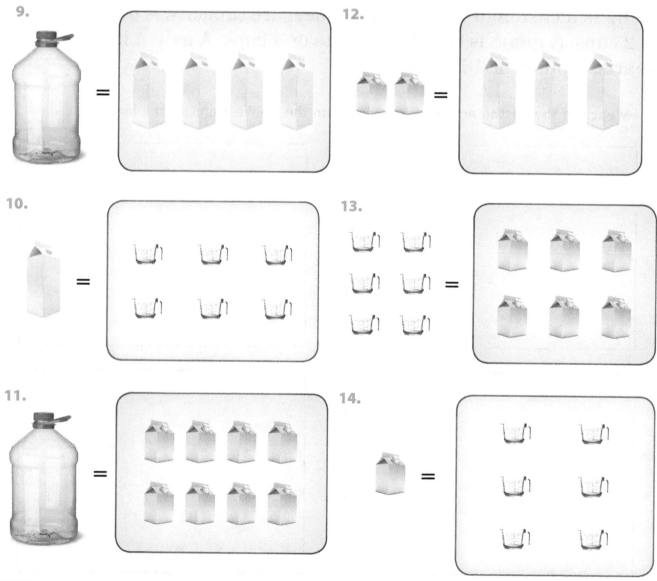

Make the amounts equal. Circle the cups, pints, or quarts as needed.

A liter is a metric unit used to measure liquids.

cup   pint   quart   liter   2 liters   gallon

Number these containers from smallest to largest.

1.

 _____    _____    _____

2.

 _____    _____    _____

3.

 _____    _____    _____

4. Circle the containers that could hold 1 liter.

Does the container hold more or less than 1 liter? Circle your answer.

5. **more** or **less**

7. **more** or **less**

6. **more** or **less**

8. **more** or **less**

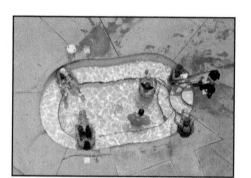

Read and follow the directions.

9. Ann drank 1 liter of water. Circle the container that holds 1 liter.

10. Felipe's family drank 1 liter of milk. Put an X on the containers that could not hold 1 liter.

Pounds and Kilograms 6.11

Circle the object that is lighter.

1.

3.

2.

4.

Circle the object that will balance the scales.

5.

6.

7. **Circle the scale you could use to weigh yourself.**

A pound is a customary unit used to measure weight.

These are things that weigh about 1 pound. Draw one more.

8.

A kilogram is a metric unit used to measure weight.

These are things that weigh about 1 kilogram. Draw one more.

9.

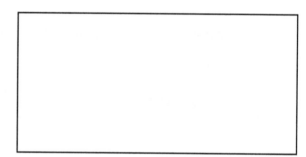

Does the object weigh more or less than 1 pound? Circle your answer.

10.  more   or   less

12.  more   or   less

11.  more   or   less

13.  more   or   less

Name _____

A degree is a unit of measurement for temperature.

Write the temperature shown on the thermometer.

1. 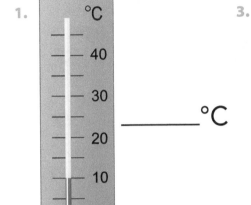 _____ °C

3. 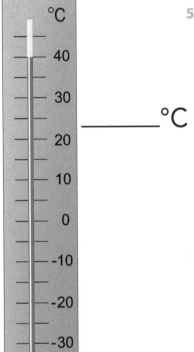 _____ °C

5. 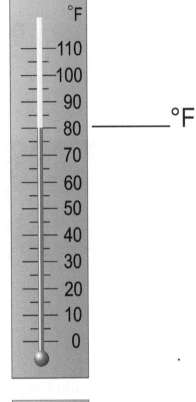 _____ °F

2. 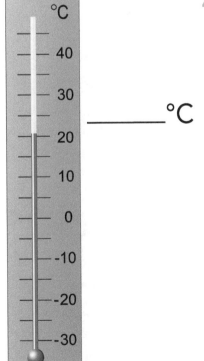 _____ °C

4. 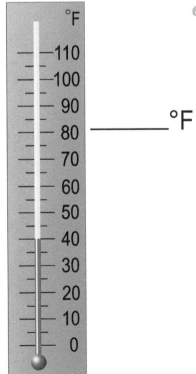 _____ °F

6. 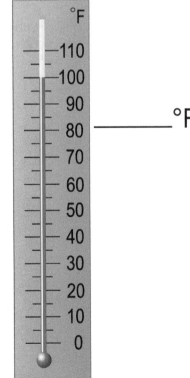 _____ °F

7. Circle the thermometers that use °F.

8. Color to show the temperature.

60°F

30°C

Choose the Best Tool 6.13

1. Match the picture to the tool you would use to measure its length.

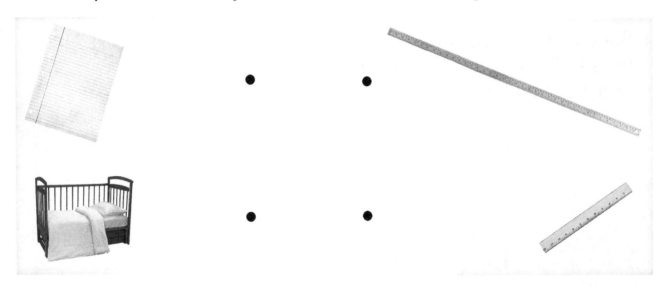

2. Match the picture to the tool you would use to measure its temperature.

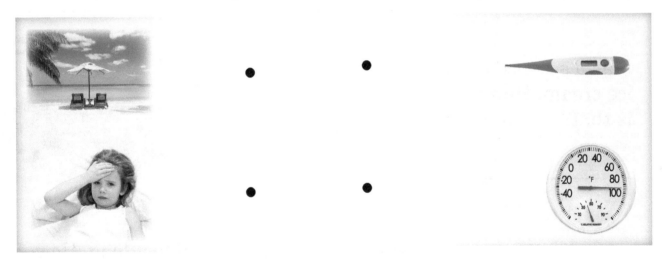

3. Match the picture to the tool you would use to measure its weight.

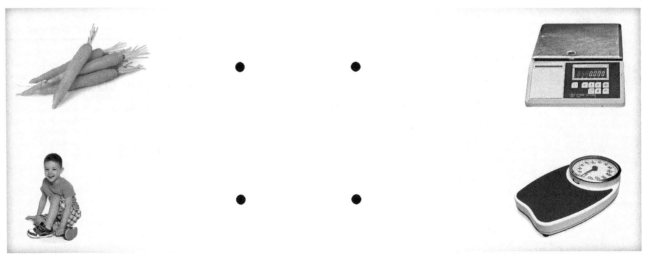

Read and answer each question.

4. Sade needs 6 cups of flour to make bread. Should she use a 1 pint bowl or a 1 gallon bowl?

_____

5. Dan has a hose that is 14 feet long. Is his hose longer or shorter than 2 yards? 1 yard = 3 feet

_____

6. Maria scooped out 2 pints of ice cream. How many cups is that? 1 pint = 2 cups

_____

7. Tito made a line that is 6 feet long. How many yards is that? 3 feet = 1 yard

_____

Is Tito's line longer or shorter than 36 inches long? 1 yard = 36 inches

longer   or   shorter

Measure each line in inches. Circle the longest.

1.

_____ inches

2.

_____ inches

3.

_____ inches

Measure each line in centimeters. Circle the longest.

4. _____ centimeters

5. _____ centimeters

6. _____ centimeters

Number these containers from largest to smallest.

7.

2 liters   cup   gallon   pint   quart

_____   _____   _____   _____   _____

8. Draw lines to match the words to the correct shapes.

cone   sphere   cylinder   cube

9. You have to give your dog a bath. What container would help you fill the tub the fastest? Circle it.

gallon

pint

cup

10. What tool would help you measure the playground the fastest? Circle it.

11. Fill in the circle that shows the temperature.

○ 60°F

○ 10°C

○ 0°F

○ 10°C

○ 60°F

○ 40°C

12. Circle the item that weighs about one kilogram.

Solve.

1.
```
   4
+  3
```
□

3.
```
   2
+  7
```
□

5.
```
   5
+  1
```
□

7.
```
   26
+ 13
```
□

9.
```
   76
+ 23
```
□

2.
```
   10
-   5
```
□

4.
```
   7
-  6
```
□

6.
```
   8
-  4
```
□

8.
```
   48
- 25
```
□

10.
```
   49
- 27
```
□

11. $11 - 4 =$ _____

12. $7 + 3 =$ _____

13. $11 - 3 =$ _____

Write the value of the coins.

14.     = _____ ¢

15.   = _____ ¢

16.    = _____ ¢

17. Write the number with 4 in the tens place and 0 in the ones place. _____

18. What number has the highest value in the tens place? Circle it.

156   561   615

Write the time.

19.

•
•
_____

20.

•
•
_____

21.

•
•
_____

22.

•
•
_____

23. **Circle the longest cone.**

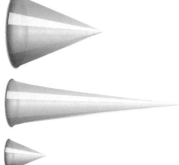

24. **Circle the shortest cylinder.**

Measure each picture.

25.

_____ inches

26. _____

_____ centimeters

27. Sari's Bible class will have art day. Each child needs 1 cup of finger paint. There are 8 children. How many quarts of paint do they need? 1 quart = 4 cups

_____ quarts

Draw cups. Circle sets of 4.

Chapter 7
Using Numbers to 100

How precious to me are Your thoughts, God!
How vast is the sum of them! Were I to count
them, they would outnumber the grains
of sand—when I awake,
I am still with You.
Psalm 139:17–18

Key Ideas:

Addition: basic facts to 12, adding three addends

Subtraction: basic facts to 12

Number Theory: order numbers to 100

Place Value: using place value to add and subtract

Algebra: finding missing addends

Connect the dots. Color.

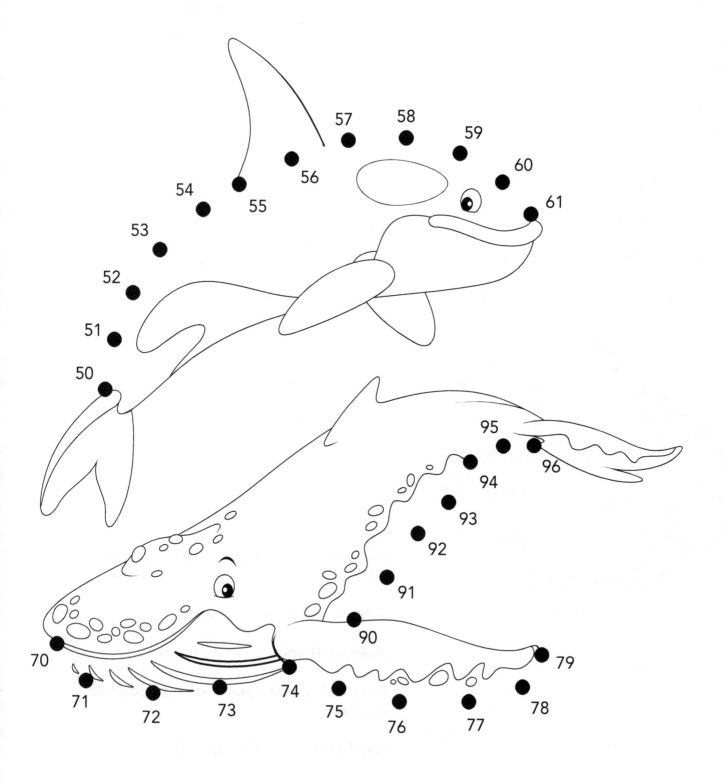

Fill in the circle if the picture shows 100 in any way.

1.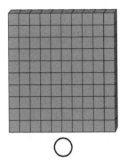
   ○

2.
   ○

3.
   ○

4.
   ○

5.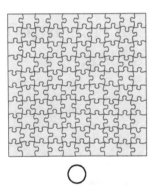
   ○

6.
   ○

7.
   ○

8.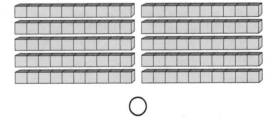
   ○

9. Trace the number words.

10. Check the box for each activity that you complete.

☐ Make a train of 100 connecting cubes.

☐ Count to 100.

☐ Go outside and take 100 steps. Have a friend step next to you. See whose steps are longer.

☐ Stamp your thumbprint 100 times.

☐ Sit quietly for 100 seconds.

☐ Read some words from Psalm 100.

☐ Use a hundred chart to count to 100 by 5s and 10s.

☐ Do 100 jumping jacks.

☐ Clap your hands 100 times.

☐ Draw 100 circles.

☐ Cut a piece of ribbon 100 centimeters long.

11. Are there more or less than 100 penguins? Circle your answer.

more than 100   less than 100

Write the fact families for each picture.

1.

___ + ___ = ___

___ + ___ = ___

___ − ___ = ___

___ − ___ = ___

3.

___ + ___ = ___

___ − ___ = ___

2.

___ + ___ = ___

___ + ___ = ___

___ − ___ = ___

___ − ___ = ___

4.

___ + ___ = ___

___ + ___ = ___

___ − ___ = ___

___ − ___ = ___

Complete the fact families.

5.

$$\begin{array}{r} 2 \\ + 3 \\ \hline \end{array}$$
$$\begin{array}{r} 3 \\ + 2 \\ \hline \end{array}$$

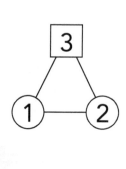

$$\begin{array}{r} 5 \\ - \bigcirc \\ \hline \end{array}$$
$$\begin{array}{r} 5 \\ - \bigcirc \\ \hline \end{array}$$

6.

$$\begin{array}{r} 1 \\ + 2 \\ \hline \end{array}$$
$$\begin{array}{r} \\ + \bigcirc \\ \hline \end{array}$$

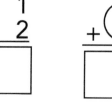

$$\begin{array}{r} 3 \\ - \bigcirc \\ \hline \end{array}$$
$$\begin{array}{r} 3 \\ - \bigcirc \\ \hline \end{array}$$

Match the number sentence to the answer.

7. 1 + 2 =   3 + 1 =   6 + 0 =   **8.** 5 − 3 =   1 + 4 =   6 − 5 =
   •   •   •   •   •   •

   •   •   •   •   •   •
   4   6   3   1   2   5

Write the math problem for each picture.

9.

_____

+ _____

10.

_____

+ _____

Add.

1.

$+\ \dfrac{4}{7}$

2.

$+\ \dfrac{7}{2}$

3.

$+\ \dfrac{3}{4}$

Subtract.

4.

$-\ \dfrac{10}{2}$

5.

$-\ \dfrac{12}{6}$

6.

$-\ \dfrac{7}{4}$

Draw cherries to make 11 in each set.

7.

8.

9.

Draw cherries to make 12 in each set.

10.

11.

12.

Mark off to subtract. Write the difference.

13.

$12 - 1 = $ _____

14.

$12 - 2 = $ _____

15.

$12 - 3 = $ _____

Mark off to subtract. Write the difference. Do you see a pattern?

16.

$12 - 4 = $ _____

17.

$12 - 5 = $ _____

18.

$12 - 6 = $ _____

Subtract. Write the number sentence.

19.

$11 - $ ____ $ = $ ____

20.

$12 - $ ____ $ = $ ____

21.

$11 - $ ____ $ = $ ____

22.

$11 - $ ____ $ = $ ____

23. Draw whole apples and cores to show the subtraction sentence.

$12 - 7 = 5$

Color and add.

1. 2 + 3 + 3 = ____

2.
```
    0
    7
  + 2
  ┌───┐
  │   │
  └───┘
```


Circle the coins. Add.

3. 7¢ + 4¢ + 1¢ = ____ ¢

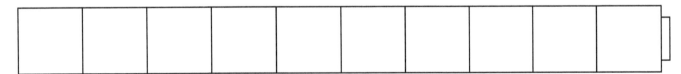

4. 2¢ + 3¢ + 5¢ = ____ ¢

5. 4¢ + 6¢ + 1¢ = ____ ¢

Add.

6. $4 + 1 + 3 = $ ____

8. $5 + 2 + 4 = $ ____

7. $1 + 4 + 3 = $ ____

9. $2 + 5 + 4 = $ ____

10.
$$
\begin{array}{r}
7 \\
2 \\
+\ 3 \\
\hline
\boxed{12}
\end{array}
$$
> 9 count on

12.
$$
\begin{array}{r}
6 \\
1 \\
+\ 2 \\
\hline
\boxed{}
\end{array}
$$

11.
$$
\begin{array}{r}
2 \\
7 \\
+\ 3 \\
\hline
\boxed{}
\end{array}
$$

13.
$$
\begin{array}{r}
1 \\
6 \\
+\ 2 \\
\hline
\boxed{}
\end{array}
$$

Review

14. Write the time shown on the first clock. Draw the hands on the second clock to show 1 hour and 15 minutes later.

Solve. Write the answers in the circles.

1.
$$\begin{array}{r} 5 \\ + \bigcirc \\ \hline 9 \end{array}$$

3.
$$\begin{array}{r} 10 \\ + \bigcirc \\ \hline 12 \end{array}$$

5. $1 + 2 + \bigcirc = 10$

6. $2 + 4 + \bigcirc = 8$

2.
$$\begin{array}{r} 3 \\ + \bigcirc \\ \hline 7 \end{array}$$

4.
$$\begin{array}{r} 7 \\ + \bigcirc \\ \hline 12 \end{array}$$

7. $2 + 4 + \bigcirc = 12$

8. Match the addends to the number sentence.

8 •

5 •

4 •

7 •

• $0 + 1 + \bigcirc = 8$

• $2 + \bigcirc + 1 = 11$

• $4 + 2 + \bigcirc = 10$

• $\bigcirc + 3 + 4 = 12$

9. Circle the number of sharks needed to complete the number sentence.

$$9 + \bigcirc + 2 = 12$$

Read and answer the questions.

10. Carlos has 10 cars. There are 2 on the race track and 1 by his elbow. The rest are in the toy box. How many cars are in the toy box?

$2 + 1 + \bigcirc = 10$

_____ cars

11. Skyler found 2 dimes. He needs 25¢ to buy an apple. How much more money does he need to find?

_____ ¢

12. Jeannie picked up 2 pebbles at the beach. She put them in a pile. Shane added 4. Teo added some too. The pile had 10 pebbles in all. How many pebbles did Teo add?

_____ pebbles

1. Color the 40s green.
2. Color the 50s blue.
3. Color the 60s red.

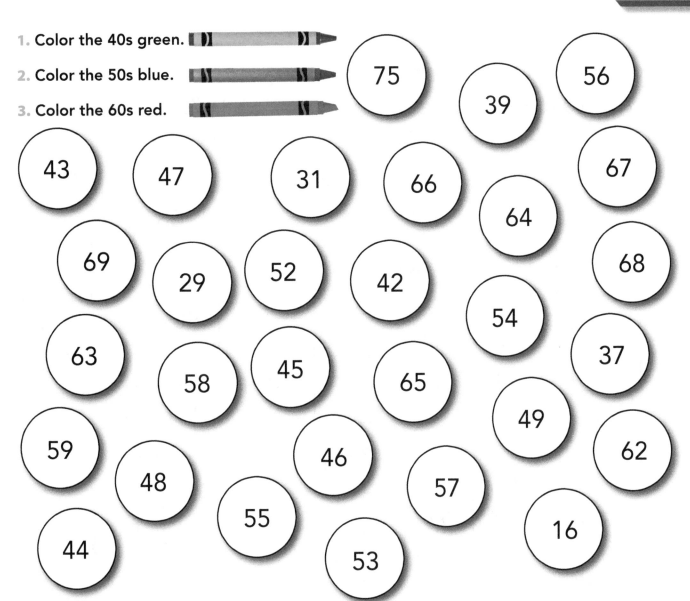

Write the missing numbers.

4.

41 | | | | | | | | 50

5.

51 | | | | | | | | 60

6.

61 | | | | | | | | 70

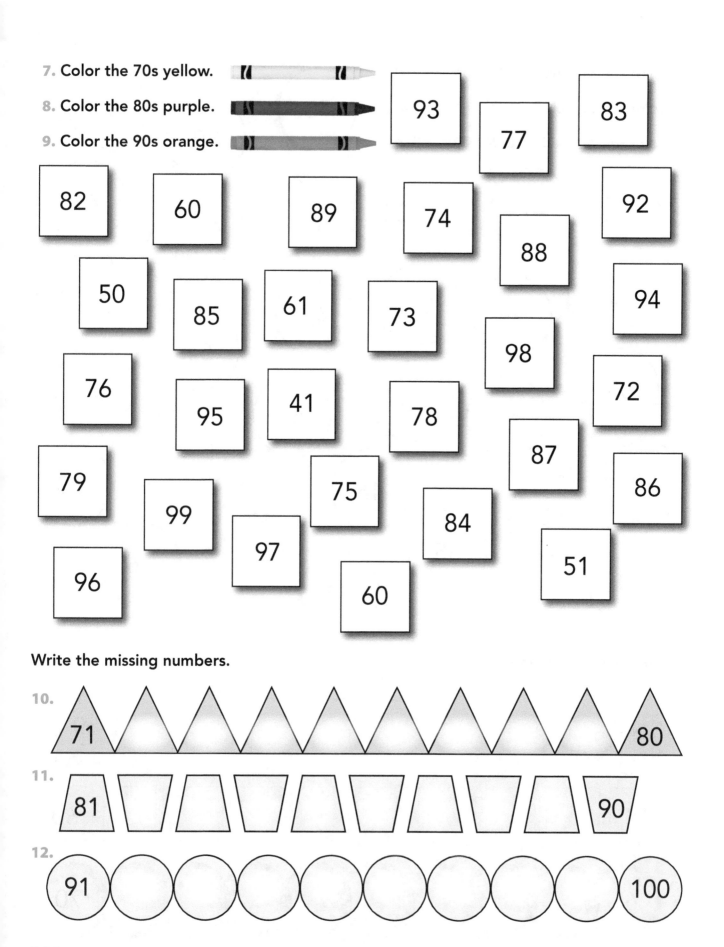

7. Color the 70s yellow.

8. Color the 80s purple.

9. Color the 90s orange.

93
77
83

82
60
89
74
92

88

50
85
61
73
94

98

76
95
41
78
72

87

79
99
75
84
86

97
51

96
60

Write the missing numbers.

10.
71 80

11.
81 90

12.
91 100

Cut out the tens. Glue them in place. Write the total number of tens and ones.

1.

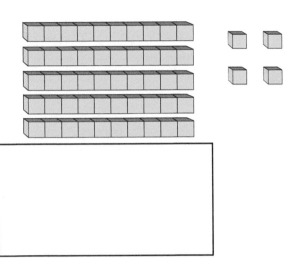

tens	ones

3.

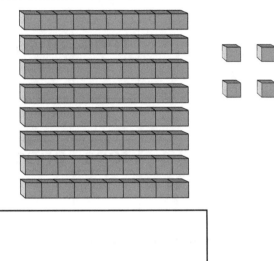

tens	ones

2.

tens	ones

4.

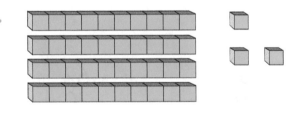

tens	ones

✂ ┄┄┄┄┄┄┄┄┄┄┄┄┄┄┄┄┄┄┄┄┄┄┄┄┄┄┄┄

Add.

5.

tens	ones

$+$ $=$

tens	ones

6.

tens	ones

$+$ $=$

tens	ones

7. **Write the missing numbers.**

32	42			72	

Add.

8. $\begin{array}{r} 50 \\ +10 \\ \hline \end{array}$

9. $\begin{array}{r} 62 \\ +20 \\ \hline \end{array}$

10. $\begin{array}{r} 64 \\ +10 \\ \hline \end{array}$

11. $\begin{array}{r} 82 \\ +10 \\ \hline \end{array}$

12. $72 + 10 =$ _____

13. $24 + 10 =$ _____

14. $11 + 20 =$ _____

Use the number line.

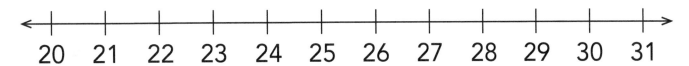

```
20  21  22  23  24  25  26  27  28  29  30  31
```

1. Start at 27. Jump forward 3. Land on _____.

2. Start at 31. Jump back 10. Land on _____.

3. Start at 25. Jump forward 5. Land on _____.

Use the number line. Circle the correct word. Fill in the blank.

4. Start at 28. Jump (back, forward) 3 spaces to a larger number.

   Land on _____.

5. Start at 29. Jump (back, forward) 4 spaces to a smaller number.

   Land on _____.

Write the number.

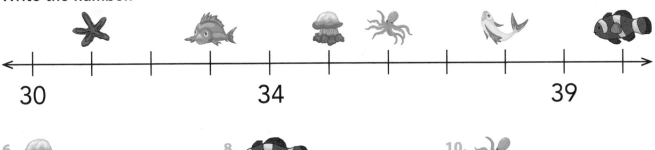

```
30              34              39
```

6.  _____

7.  _____

8.  _____

9.  _____

10.  _____

11.  _____

12. Count on. Start at 50. Color the sea animal.

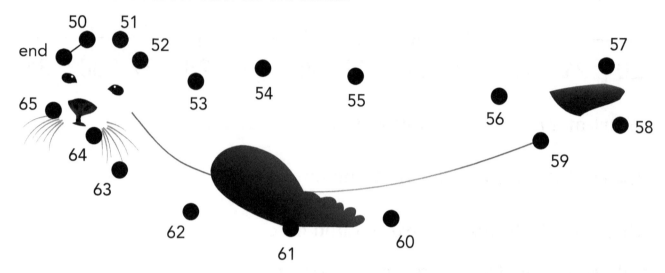

13. Count back. Start at 50. Color the sea animal.

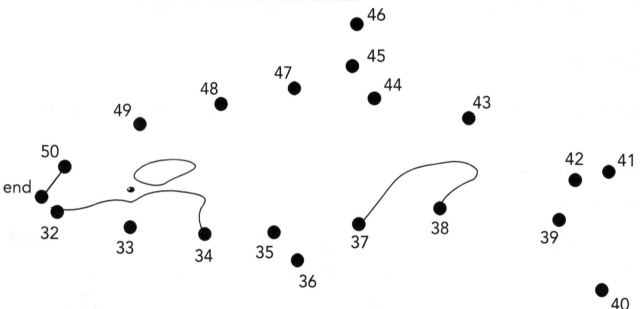

Review

Subtract.

14.
$$\begin{array}{r} 12 \\ -\ 7 \\ \hline \end{array}$$

15.
$$\begin{array}{r} 12 \\ -\ 5 \\ \hline \end{array}$$

16.
$$\begin{array}{r} 12 \\ -\ 6 \\ \hline \end{array}$$

17.
$$\begin{array}{r} 12 \\ -\ 8 \\ \hline \end{array}$$

18.
$$\begin{array}{r} 12 \\ -\ 4 \\ \hline \end{array}$$

Name _____

Read each word problem. Show the hops on the number line to solve each problem. Write the answer on the line.

1. Perry Penguin takes steps that are 2 units long. If he starts walking at 4 on the number line, where will he be after 7 steps?

_____

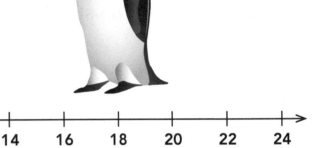

```
←—+——+——+——+——+——+——+——+——+——+——+——+——→
   2   4   6   8  10  12  14  16  18  20  22  24
       ★
     start
```

2. Fred Fox walks across the snow. His steps are 10 units each. If Fred starts walking when he is at 30, what number will he be on after 4 steps?

_____

```
←—+——+——+——+——+——+——+——+——+——+——+——→
  10  20  30  40  50  60  70  80  90 100 110
      ★
    start
```

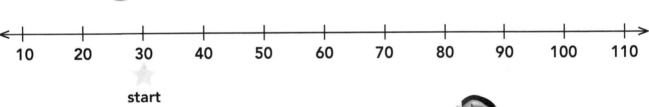

3. Penny Puffin's steps are 5 units long. Penny starts to walk at 25. She takes 5 steps. Where is she now?

_____

```
←—+——+——+——+——+——+——+——+——+——+——+——+——→
   5  10  15  20  25  30  35  40  45  50  55  60  65
                  ★
                start
```

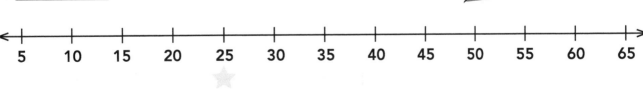

Read each word problem. Show the hops on the number line to solve each problem. Write the answer on the line.

4. Pat Polar Bear walks along the ice. Each of his steps is 10 units. If Pat starts at 20 and takes 6 steps, where will he stop?

_____

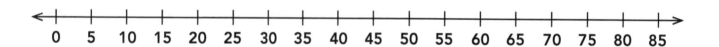

0 5 10 15 20 25 30 35 40 45 50 55 60 65 70 75 80 85

5. Walter Walrus takes steps that are 1 unit each. Walter starts at 2 and takes 7 steps. Where does Walter stop?

_____

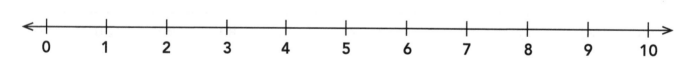

0 1 2 3 4 5 6 7 8 9 10

6. Kelly Killer Whale leaps forward in the water. She can leap 2 units at a time. Kelly starts at 0 and leaps 5 times. Where is Kelly now?

_____

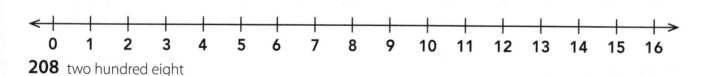

0 1 2 3 4 5 6 7 8 9 10 11 12 13 14 15 16

Count. Write the number. Circle the number that is more.

1. 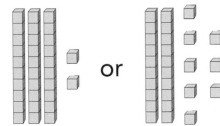   or

2. 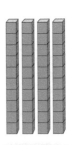   or

Count. Write the number. Circle the number that is less.

3. 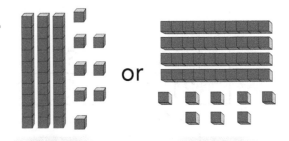   or

4.   or

Circle sets of 10. Write each number of tens and ones. Then write the numbers in order.

5.

tens	ones

6.

tens	ones

7.

tens	ones

8.

9. Take the penguin to the fish. Travel through the maze so that each number is more than the last one.

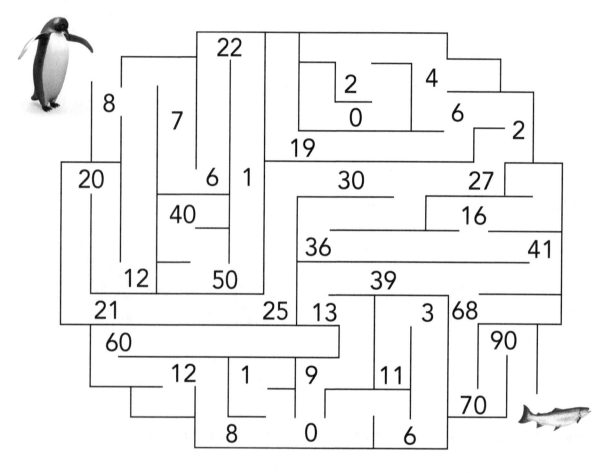

Write the numbers. In each pair, circle the number that is more.

10. 3 tens and 2 ones _____   4 tens and 0 ones _____

11. 2 tens and 5 ones _____   5 tens and 2 ones _____

12. 8 tens and 3 ones _____   3 tens and 8 ones _____

13. Write the numbers on the penguins in order.

_____ _____ _____ _____ _____ _____

Greater Than and Less Than 7.11

This is Freddy Fish. He is always hungry. He likes to eat

BIG numbers and *BIG* groups.

Trace Freddy Fish. Trace his mouth in red and his body in pencil.

1.

2.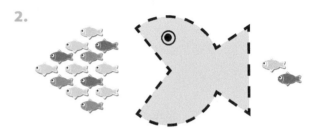

Circle the group that Freddy will eat.

3.  or

5.  or

4.  or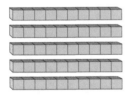

6. 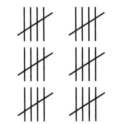 or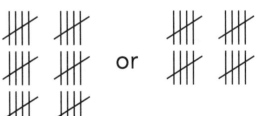

Draw Freddy Fish. Face him toward the greater number. The first one is done for you.

7. 14   39   10. 80   81

8. 72   94   11. 67   45

9. 58   20   12. 92   29

This symbol means **greater than**. > Greater than means a number or amount is more than another number or amount.

This symbol means **less than**. < Less than means a number or amount is smaller than another number or amount.

Write > or <.

13. 7 ◯ 9   15. 16 ◯ 15   17. 62 ◯ 26

14. 11 ◯ 20   16. 44 ◯ 41   18. 52 ◯ 54

Write the sum or difference. Compare the answers. Draw Freddy Fish. The first one is done for you.

19. 3 + 4 9 + 1   22. 10 − 5   3 − 0

   ◯   ◯   ◯   ◯

20. 5 + 3   2 + 2   23. 8 − 4   7 − 2

   ◯   ◯   ◯   ◯

21. 7 + 0   1 + 7   24. 5 − 3   2 − 2

   ◯   ◯   ◯   ◯

Name _____

Draw a picture to help you solve each word problem. Circle the correct answer. The first one is done for you.

1. Pedro Penguin ate 3 fish one day. He ate 2 fish the next day. Alma Penguin ate 4 fish one day. She ate 2 fish the next day. Did Pedro eat more fish than Alma?

   yes   (no)

2. Gabe and Sun Yoo went whale watching. Gabe saw 4 whales. Sun Yoo saw 6 whales. The number of whales that Gabe saw was _____ the number that Sun Yoo saw.

   greater than   less than

3. Luz saw 5 sea turtle nests. Each nest held 10 eggs. The number of eggs that Luz saw was _____ 70 eggs.

   greater than   less than

4. Count the penguins. Color one rectangle on the graph for each penguin.

Penguins

Use the graph to solve the word problems.

5. How many large penguins are there? _____

6. How many small penguins are there? _____

7. How many penguins are there in all? Write the tens and ones.

tens	ones

8. The number of large penguins is _____ the number of small penguins.

greater than   less than

Look at the signs.

greater than	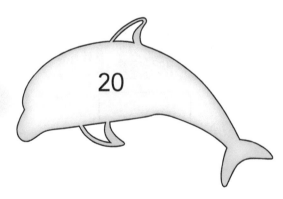	>
less than		<
equal to	=	

Write > or <.

1. 71 ____ 17

2. 41 ____ 14

3. 20 ____ 22

4. 45 ____ 54

5. 62 ____ 26

6. 20 ____ 30

7. 186 ____ 168

8. 124 ____ 142

Write >, <, or =.

9.

2 tens 0 ones   20

10.

3 tens and 9 ones   93

Write the sum or difference. Write >, <, or =.

11. $\boxed{2 + 0}$ $\boxed{1 + 2}$

_____

13. $\boxed{8 + 2}$ $\boxed{5 + 5}$

_____

12. $\boxed{7 - 4}$ $\boxed{3 + 1}$

_____

14. $\boxed{4 + 4}$ $\boxed{10 - 3}$

_____

Write a number to make each number sentence true.

15. $51 >$ _____

17. $72 <$ _____

19. $61 <$ _____

16. $90 <$ _____

18. $32 >$ _____

20. $27 >$ _____

Write the numbers. Circle > or <.

21.

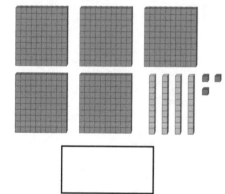

>

<

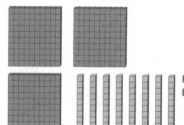

22.

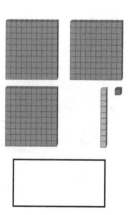

>

<

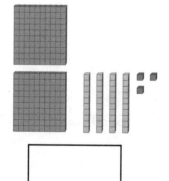

Add. Start with the ones.

1.

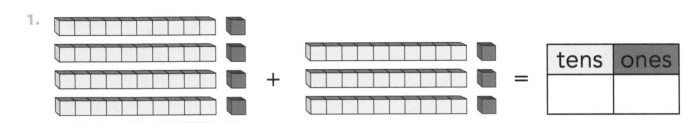

tens	ones

2.

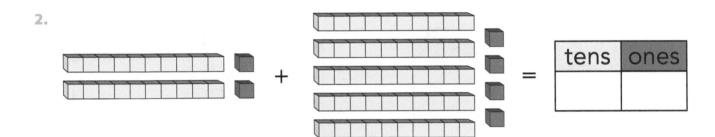

tens	ones

Write the addends. Add. Start with the ones.

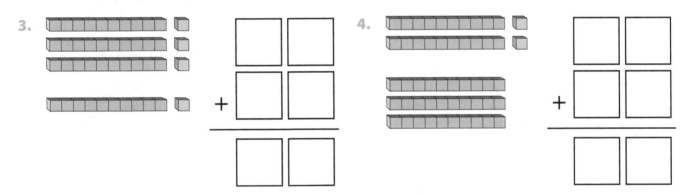

3.

+

4.

+

Cross off to subtract. Start with the ones. Write the difference.

5.

− 2 1

6.

− 5 3

© *Mathematics* Grade 1

Add or subtract. Start with the ones.

7.

hundreds	tens	ones
▦	‖‖	⠿⠿

8.

hundreds	tens	ones
▦ ▦ ▦	‖‖‖‖	⠲⠂

+

hundreds	tens	ones
▦ ▦	‖‖‖‖	⠐⠂

−

hundreds	tens	ones
▦ ▦			⠄

Write the number.

9. 200 + 30 + 2 =

hundreds	tens	ones

10. 100 + 80 + 7 =

hundreds	tens	ones

Review

11. Circle numbers less than 50. Cross out numbers greater than 100.

5   21   36   45   7   39   53   182   159   40   61   33   86

Name _____

Write the missing numbers.

1. __10__ __15__ __20__ _____ _____ _____

2. __80__ __70__ __60__ _____ _____ _____

3. __22__ __24__ _____ __28__ __30__ _____ _____ __36__

4. __94__ __93__ __92__ _____ _____ _____

5. __70__ _____ __68__ _____ __66__ _____ _____ _____

Use the number line. Show the hops.

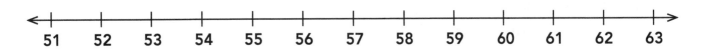

| 51 | 52 | 53 | 54 | 55 | 56 | 57 | 58 | 59 | 60 | 61 | 62 | 63 |

6. Start at 59.
   Take 3 hops forward.

   You land on _____.

7. Start at 56.
   Hop back 4 spaces.

   You land on _____.

Write the number.

8.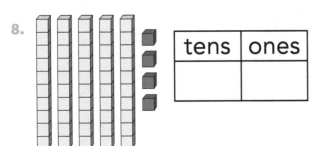

tens	ones

9.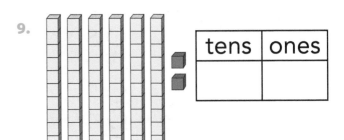

tens	ones

Add.

10. $4 + 1 + 7 =$ _____

11. $4 + 4 + 3 =$ _____

12. Count on to solve the word problem.

Susie Seagull flies over the number line.
She flies 5 units at a time before she lands.
If she starts at 0, where will she land after
2 flights?

_____

0   5   10   15   20   25   30   35   40

13. Draw a picture to solve the word problem.

Rayna has 3 dimes.
Mara has 4 pennies.
How much money do
they have in all?

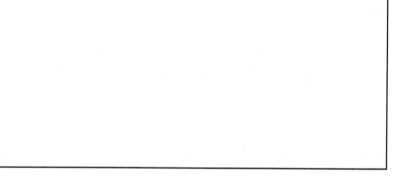

_____ ¢

Fill in the circle in front of the correct answer.

14.

$4 + \underline{\quad} = 12$
- ○ 8
- ○ 9
- ○ 5

16.

$5 + \underline{\quad} = 12$
- ○ 7
- ○ 8
- ○ 9

15.

$9 + \underline{\quad} = 12$
- ○ 5
- ○ 4
- ○ 3

17.

$6 + \underline{\quad} = 12$
- ○ 5
- ○ 6
- ○ 7

Write >, <, or =.

18. $25 \underline{\quad} 47$

19. $61 \underline{\quad} 61$

20. $75 \underline{\quad} 70$

Chapter 8
Fractions

Taking the five loaves and the two fish and looking up to heaven, He gave thanks and broke the loaves. Then He gave them to the disciples, and the disciples gave them to the people.
Matthew 14:19b

Key Ideas:

Fractions: identifying equal parts, halves, thirds, and fourths

Fractions: identifying halves, thirds, and fourths of a set

Fractions: reading and writing fractions

Fractions: solving fraction-related word problems

Color the fraction $\frac{1}{2}$ red. Color $\frac{1}{3}$ green. Color $\frac{1}{4}$ orange.

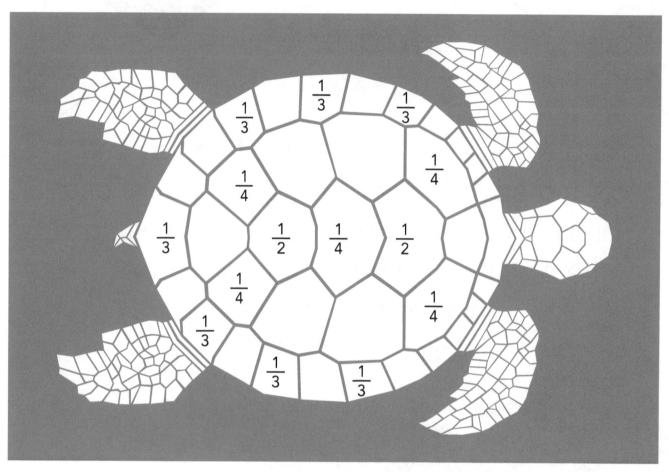

Sea Turtle Facts

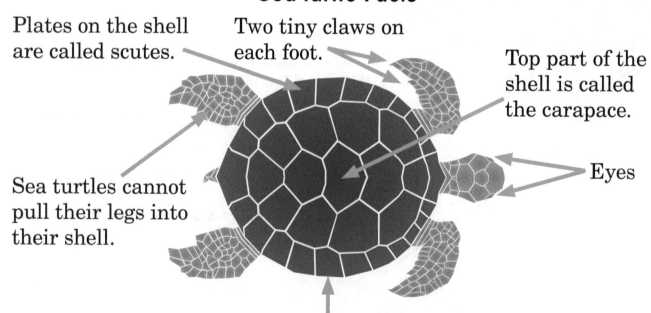

Plates on the shell are called scutes.

Two tiny claws on each foot.

Top part of the shell is called the carapace.

Sea turtles cannot pull their legs into their shell.

Eyes

Shell on the bottom is called the plastron.

A **fraction** is a part of a whole.

Circle whole **or** fraction.

1.

whole

fraction

4.

whole

fraction

7.

whole

fraction

10.

whole

fraction

2.

whole

fraction

5.

whole

fraction

8.

whole

fraction

11.

whole

fraction

3.

whole

fraction

6.

whole

fraction

9.

whole

fraction

12.

whole

fraction

Equal parts of a shape are sections that are the same size.

Fill in the circle if the foods have been cut into equal parts.

13.   ○

14.   ○

15.   ○

Color the shapes that are divided into equal parts. Color each part a different color.

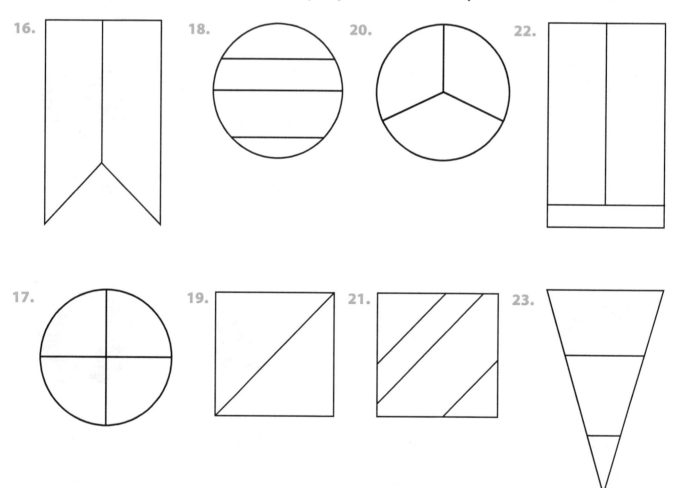

16.

18.

20.

22.

17.

19.

21.

23.

A half is one part of a whole that has been divided into two equal parts. It is written like this: $\frac{1}{2}$.

Draw a line to divide each shape into halves. Color one-half of each shape.

1.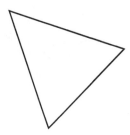

3.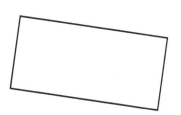

5.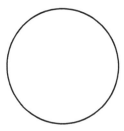

2.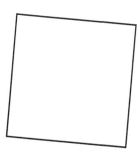

4.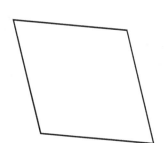

6.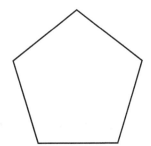

Draw a line to show halves.

7.

8.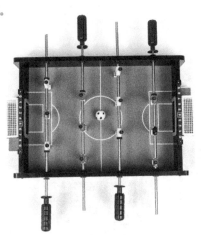

9.

10. Cross out the pictures of the moon that do not show halves.

11. Circle the correct way to write one-half.

$$\frac{2}{1} \qquad \frac{1}{2}$$

12. These circles are all divided into equal parts. Which ones show halves? Color them.

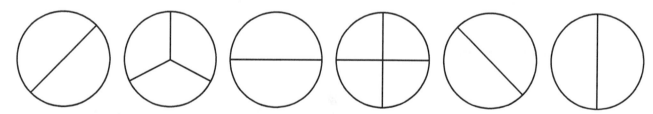

13. Circle the jar that is half full of jelly.

A third is one part of a whole that has been divided into three equal parts. It is written like this: $\frac{1}{3}$.

1. Color one-third of the shape.

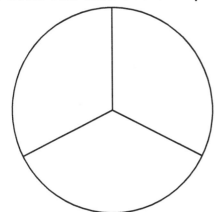

2. Color two-thirds of the shape.

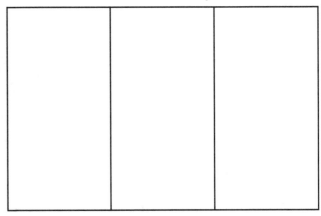

Circle the one in each pair that shows three equal parts.

3.

5.

4.

6.

Draw lines to show thirds.

7.

8.

9.

Write the number of equal parts in each shape.

10.

_____

11. 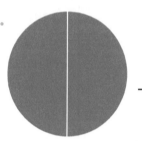 _____

12.  _____

13. What fraction of the circle is blue?

○ one-third ○ two-thirds

14. What fraction is red and yellow combined?

○ one-third ○ two-thirds

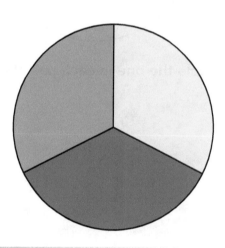

Review

15. Write the number of triangles.

_____ triangles

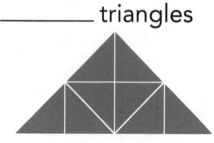

16. Circle the shapes that have symmetry.

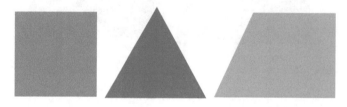

A fourth is one part of a whole that has been divided into four equal parts. It is written like this: $\frac{1}{4}$.

This square has four equal parts. Look at the colored parts.

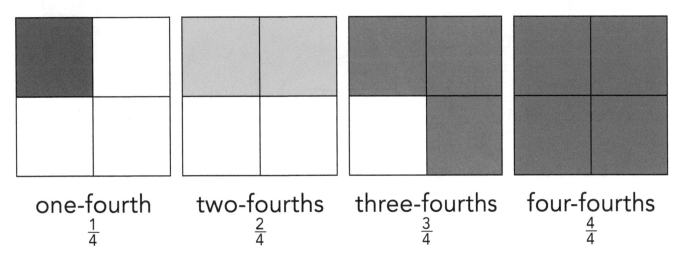

one-fourth	two-fourths	three-fourths	four-fourths
$\frac{1}{4}$	$\frac{2}{4}$	$\frac{3}{4}$	$\frac{4}{4}$

Draw lines to divide each shape into fourths.

1.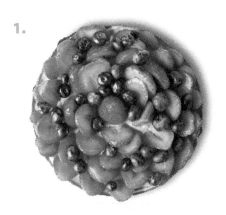

2.

3.

4. Draw a smiley face under the kite that shows only one-fourth colored.

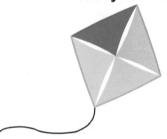 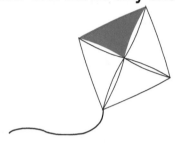 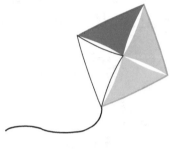

_____ _____ _____

Circle the fraction that shows the colored part.

5.

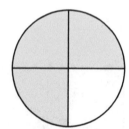

two-fourths
or
three-fourths

7.

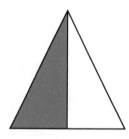

one-half
or
one-third

9.

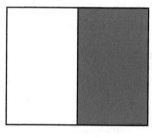

$\frac{1}{3}$ or $\frac{1}{2}$

6.

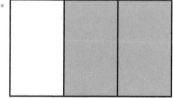

two-thirds
or
three-fourths

8.

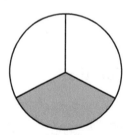

one-third
or
two-thirds

10.

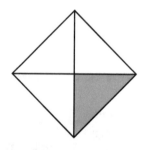

$\frac{3}{4}$ or $\frac{1}{4}$

11. Circle the picture that shows the smaller fraction.

One-half is one part of a set that can be divided into two equal parts.

Count and write.

1. Some turtles are swimming up to the top. Some turtles are swimming down. How many turtles are there in all?

   _____ turtles

2. Draw a circle around $\frac{1}{2}$ of the turtles. How many turtles did you circle?

   _____ turtles

Count the baby turtles. Draw a circle around each of the two equal sets.

3. How many baby turtles did you count in all?

   _____ turtles

4. How many baby turtles are $\frac{1}{2}$ of the turtles?

   _____ turtles

5. Draw 10 turtles on the beach. Color $\frac{1}{2}$ of the turtles.

6. Draw 6 fish in the water. Color $\frac{1}{2}$ of the fish.

7. Draw 4 clouds in the sky. Circle $\frac{1}{2}$ of the clouds.

8. How many turtles did you color? _____ turtles

9. How many fish did you color? _____ fish

10. How many clouds did you circle? _____ clouds

Color the animals to match the fraction.

1.

$$\frac{1}{3}$$

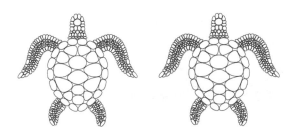

2.

$$\frac{1}{2}$$

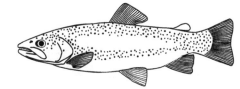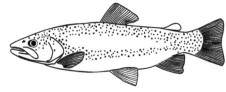

3.

$$\frac{2}{3}$$

4.

$$\frac{1}{3}$$

5.

$$\frac{1}{2}$$

6.

$$\frac{1}{3}$$

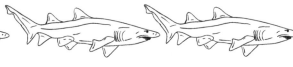

Circle one-third of the objects in each set.

7.

9.

11.

8.

10.

12.

Circle two-thirds of the objects in each set.

13.

15.

17.

14.

16.

18.

19. **Write the fraction for the colored part of the set of turtles.**

Name _____

Make the fractions with your cubes. Color the cubes below to match the fraction.

1.
$$\frac{1}{4}$$

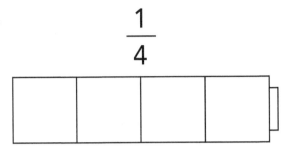

4.
$$\frac{1}{2}$$

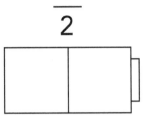

2.
$$\frac{1}{3}$$

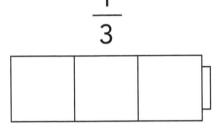

5.
$$\frac{2}{4}$$

3.
$$\frac{3}{4}$$

6.
$$\frac{2}{3}$$

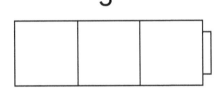

Write the fraction for the colored part of each set.

7.

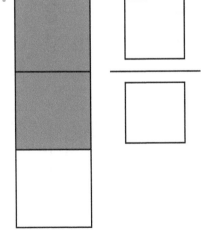

8.

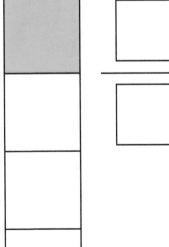

9.

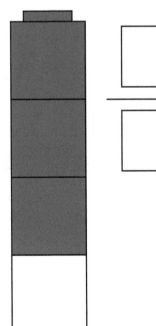

Fill in the circle that tells the fraction of brown fish.

10.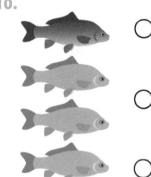
○ $\dfrac{1}{3}$

○ $\dfrac{1}{2}$

○ $\dfrac{1}{4}$

12.
○ $\dfrac{2}{3}$

○ $\dfrac{1}{3}$

○ $\dfrac{2}{1}$

14.
○ $\dfrac{3}{1}$

○ $\dfrac{3}{3}$

○ $\dfrac{3}{4}$

11.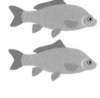
○ $\dfrac{1}{2}$

○ $\dfrac{1}{3}$

13.
○ $\dfrac{2}{3}$

○ $\dfrac{2}{4}$

○ $\dfrac{2}{2}$

15.
○ $\dfrac{1}{2}$

○ $\dfrac{2}{3}$

○ $\dfrac{1}{3}$

Review

Add or subtract.

16.
$\begin{array}{r} 6 \\ + 6 \\ \hline \end{array}$

18.
$\begin{array}{r} 4 \\ + 7 \\ \hline \end{array}$

20.
$\begin{array}{r} 10 \\ - 5 \\ \hline \end{array}$

22.
$\begin{array}{r} 9 \\ - 4 \\ \hline \end{array}$

24.
$\begin{array}{r} 3 \\ + 8 \\ \hline \end{array}$

17.
$\begin{array}{r} 7 \\ + 3 \\ \hline \end{array}$

19.
$\begin{array}{r} 12 \\ - 8 \\ \hline \end{array}$

21.
$\begin{array}{r} 6 \\ + 4 \\ \hline \end{array}$

23.
$\begin{array}{r} 11 \\ - 7 \\ \hline \end{array}$

25.
$\begin{array}{r} 11 \\ - 5 \\ \hline \end{array}$

Write the fraction for the black tile in each picture.

1.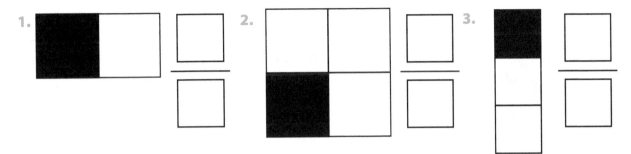

2.

3.

Write the fraction of each pizza that has been eaten.

4.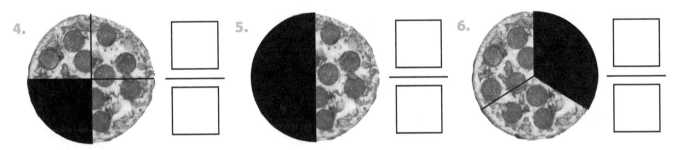

5.

6.

Draw a circle around the animals in each set to match the fraction.

7.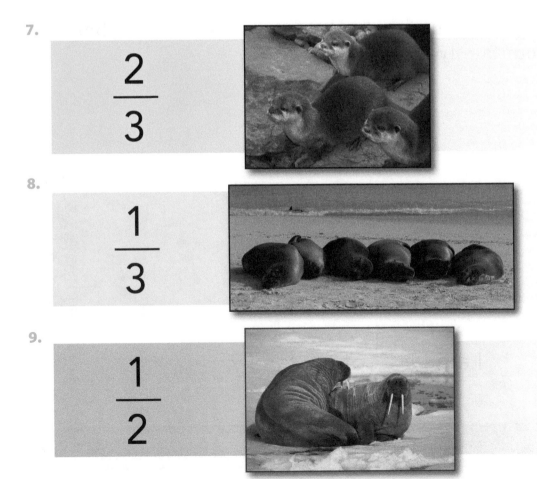

$\dfrac{2}{3}$

8.

$\dfrac{1}{3}$

9.

$\dfrac{1}{2}$

Fill in the blanks.

10. How many grapes are in the bunch? _____
If Omari pulls off 2 grapes, what fraction
of the grapes are left on the bunch?

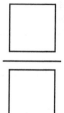

11. How many carrots are in the ground? _____
Jill takes three-fourths of them. Circle the
number of carrots she takes.

12. Draw the people in your family. Draw yourself as well. What
fraction of your family are you?

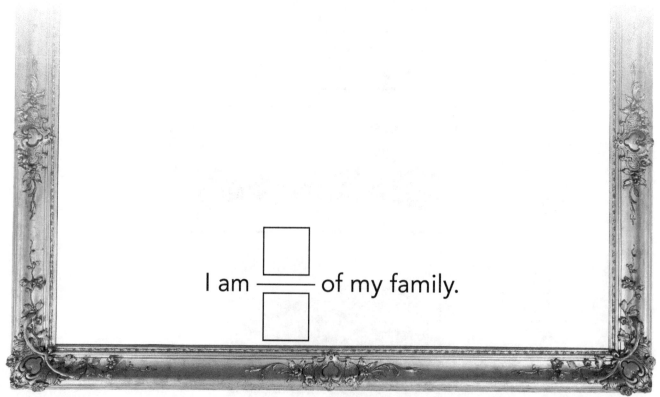

I am ⬚/⬚ of my family.

Write the fraction for the colored part.

1.

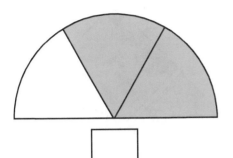

2.

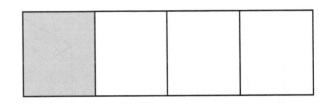

3.

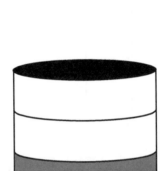

4.

5.

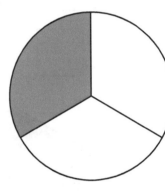

6. Write the fraction for the .

Cover the colored part with pattern blocks. Write the fraction for the colored part.

7.

8.

9.

10.

11.

Read the word problem. Color the picture to show the fraction. Write the number or fraction.

1. Ali and Mara caught 10 fish.
   One-half of the fish were green.
   How many were green?

   ____ fish

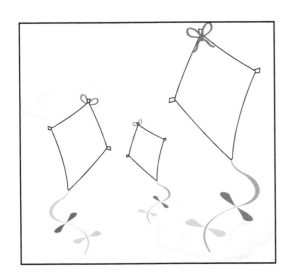

2. Jon saw 3 kites.
   One-third of the kites were red.
   How many were not red?

   ____ kites or $\dfrac{\boxed{}}{\boxed{}}$ of the kites

3. Mom broke $\frac{1}{2}$ of the 12 eggs.
   How many eggs did she break?

   ____ eggs

Read the word problems. Circle the items. Write the number or the fraction.

4. Joe saw 4 shells on the sand.
   He picked up $\frac{3}{4}$ of them.
   How many are left on the sand?

   ____ shell

5. Grant lost $\frac{1}{3}$ of his 3 pencils.
   How many does he have left?

   ____ pencils

6. Layla plays basketball. She took
   4 shots. One ball went in the basket.
   What fraction of her shots went
   into the basket?

   $\frac{\square}{\square}$ of the shots

Make each shape on the geoboard.

1. Start at the red peg. Make a rectangle that is 4 spaces long and 3 spaces high. Draw lines between all the pegs. How many small squares do you see?

   _____ squares

   Are the squares equal parts?   yes   no

2. Start at the green peg. Make a square that is 4 spaces long and 4 spaces high. Draw an up-and-down line to cut your square in half. How many unused pegs are in each half?

   _____ pegs

3. Start at the blue peg. Make a rectangle that is 7 spaces long and 2 spaces high. Draw lines from the top line through the pegs in the center of the rectangle to the bottom line. Count the small rectangles. How many small rectangles do you see?

   _____ rectangles

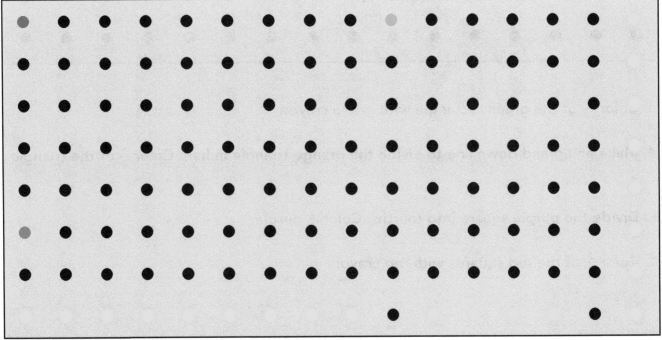

Make the shapes below on your geoboard. Use the geoboard on the page to complete the exercises.

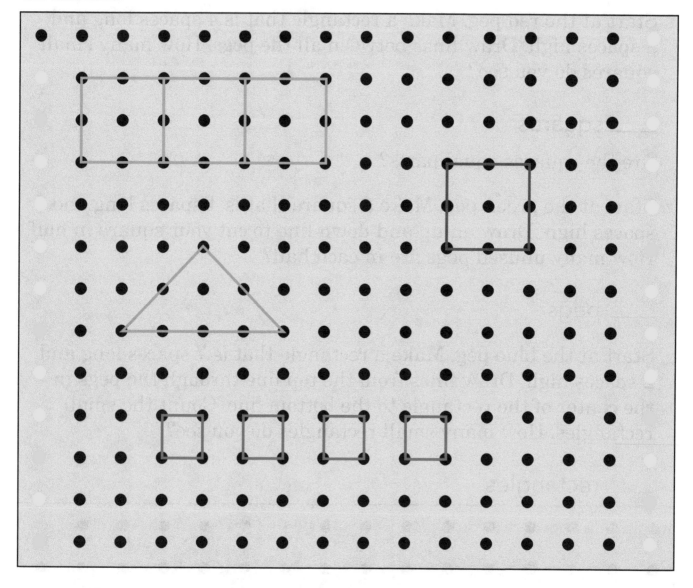

4. Color $\frac{2}{3}$ of the green rectangle with green crayon.

5. Make an up-and-down line to divide the orange triangle in half. Color $\frac{1}{2}$ of the triangle orange.

6. Divide the purple square into fourths. Color $\frac{3}{4}$ purple.

7. Color $\frac{2}{4}$ of the red squares with red crayon.

Cut and glue the piece that completes the shape.

What fractional part did you add? Circle the fraction.

1.
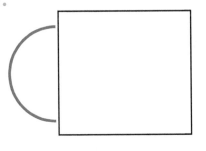

$\dfrac{1}{2}$

or

$\dfrac{1}{3}$

5.
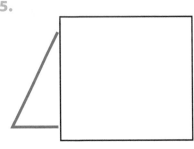

$\dfrac{1}{4}$

or

$\dfrac{1}{2}$

2.
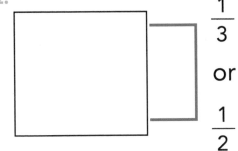

$\dfrac{1}{3}$

or

$\dfrac{1}{2}$

6.
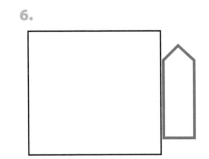

$\dfrac{1}{2}$

or

$\dfrac{3}{4}$

3.
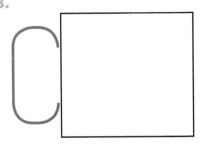

$\dfrac{2}{3}$

or

$\dfrac{2}{4}$

7.
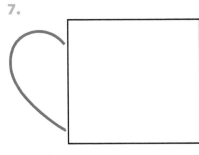

$\dfrac{1}{4}$

or

$\dfrac{1}{2}$

4.
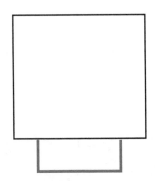

$\dfrac{3}{4}$

or

$\dfrac{1}{3}$

8.
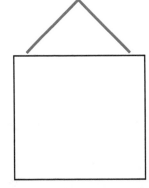

$\dfrac{1}{4}$

or

$\dfrac{1}{2}$

Circle the coins to make the fraction shown. Write the amount of money circled.

9.

$$\frac{1}{2} = \underline{\hspace{2cm}}¢$$

11.

$$\frac{3}{4} = \underline{\hspace{2cm}}¢$$

10.

$$\frac{1}{4} = \underline{\hspace{2cm}}¢$$

12.

$$\frac{2}{4} = \underline{\hspace{2cm}}¢$$

Color to show the fraction.

13.

$$\frac{3}{4}$$

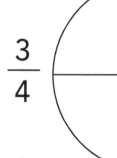

15.

$$\frac{1}{4}$$

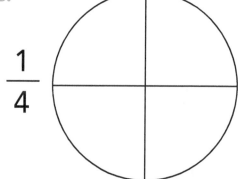

14.

$$\frac{2}{4}$$

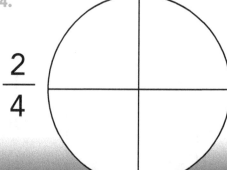

16.

$$\frac{4}{4}$$

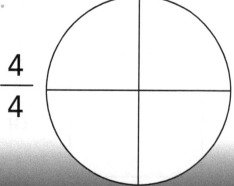

1. Color the water under $\frac{3}{4}$ of the sailboats.

2. Draw a red flag at the top of $\frac{1}{2}$ of the sailboats.

3. Draw a fish in the water near $\frac{1}{4}$ of the sailboats.

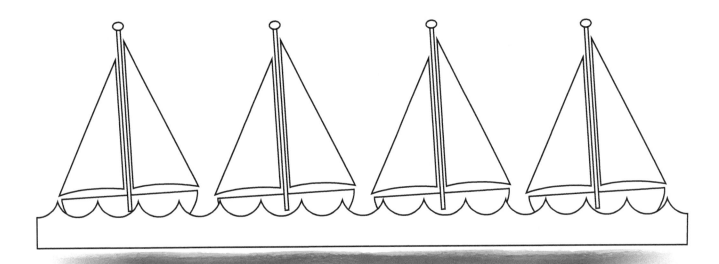

4. Color $\frac{1}{3}$ of the octopuses green.

5. Draw a smile on $\frac{2}{3}$ of the octopuses.

6. Draw water around all the octopuses.

7. Color $\frac{1}{2}$ of the fish orange.

8. Circle sets of 2 fish. How many sets did you circle? _____

   Each set is $\frac{1}{4}$ of the fish.

9. Draw water around $\frac{3}{4}$ of the fish.

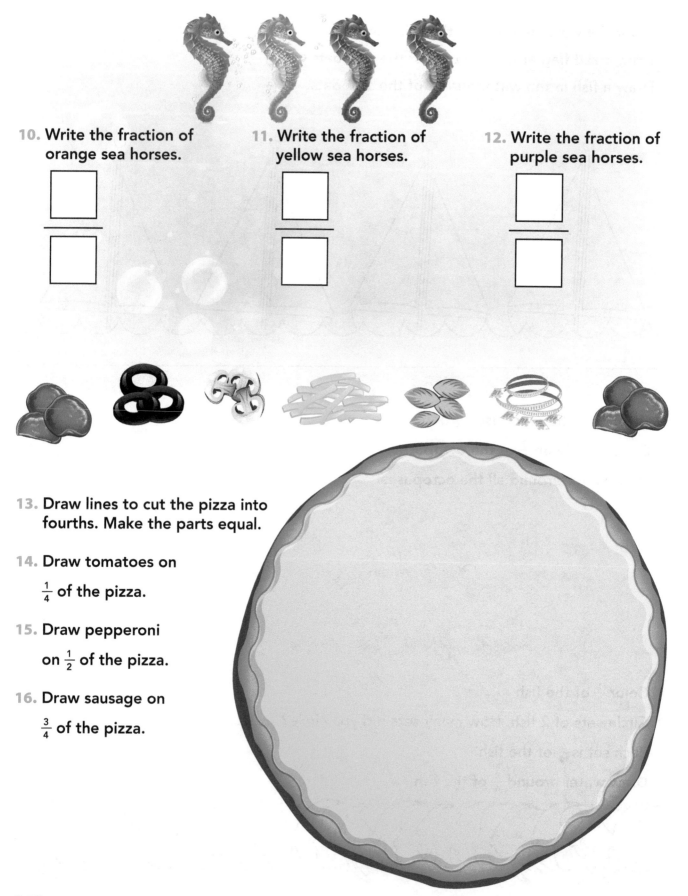

10. Write the fraction of orange sea horses.

☐
─
☐

11. Write the fraction of yellow sea horses.

☐
─
☐

12. Write the fraction of purple sea horses.

☐
─
☐

13. Draw lines to cut the pizza into fourths. Make the parts equal.

14. Draw tomatoes on $\frac{1}{4}$ of the pizza.

15. Draw pepperoni on $\frac{1}{2}$ of the pizza.

16. Draw sausage on $\frac{3}{4}$ of the pizza.

1. Circle the pictures that show only $\frac{1}{2}$ colored.

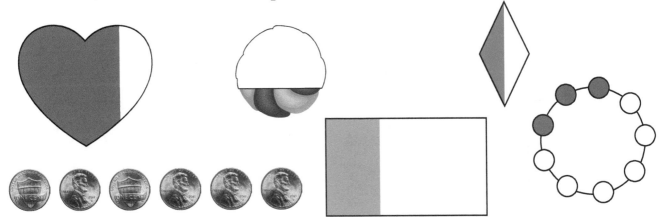

2. Circle the pictures that show only $\frac{1}{3}$ colored.

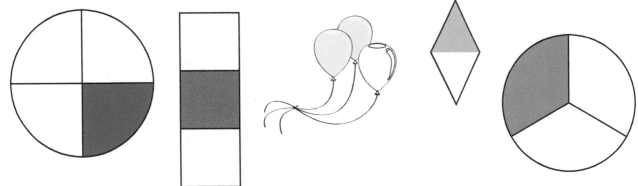

3. Circle the pictures that show only $\frac{1}{4}$ colored.

Color to show the fraction.

4. 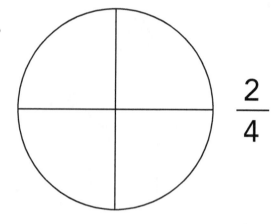 $\dfrac{2}{4}$

5. 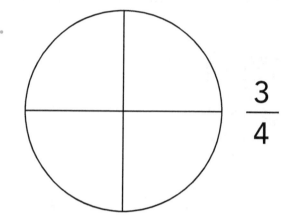 $\dfrac{3}{4}$

6. **Write the fraction of water in the cup.**

 $\dfrac{\square}{\square}$

8. **Write the fraction of juice in the bottle.**

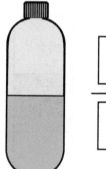 $\dfrac{\square}{\square}$

7. **Write the fraction of unbroken eggs.**

 $\dfrac{\square}{\square}$

9. **Write the fraction of spotted shells.**

   $\dfrac{\square}{\square}$

10. Joel has 6 toy cars. He took a third of them to school. How many did he take? Draw a picture.

_____ cars

Chapter 9
Two- and Three-Digit Numbers

Let heaven and earth praise Him,
the seas and all that move in them.
Psalm 69:34

Key Ideas:

Addition: adding two- and three-digit numbers

Subtraction: subtracting two- and three-digit numbers

Place Value: using place value to add and subtract

Color. Use the key.

Numerals with a 5 in the tens place =

Numerals with a 5 in the ones place =

1. Add and color.

7 = ▬▬▬▬
8 = ▬▬▬▬
9 = ▬▬▬▬
10 = ▬▬▬▬
11 = ▬▬▬▬
12 = ▬▬▬▬

7 + 5

9 + 2

6 + 6

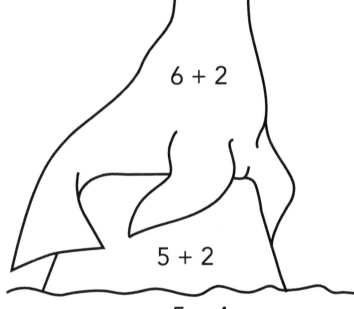

6 + 2

5 + 3

5 + 2

3 + 4

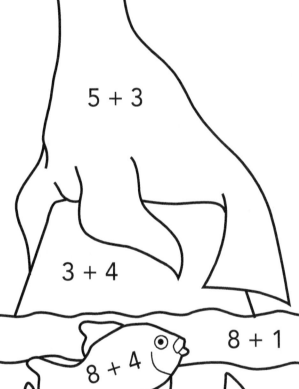

5 + 4

8 + 1

8 + 4

8 + 2

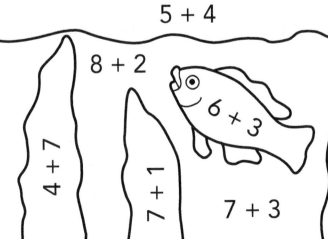

6 + 3

4 + 7

7 + 1

7 + 3

8 + 3

9 + 1

5 + 6

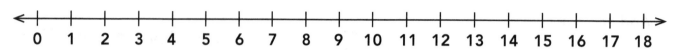

0 1 2 3 4 5 6 7 8 9 10 11 12 13 14 15 16 17 18

Solve. Draw pictures, use tallies, or count on the number line to check your answers.

2.
$$\begin{array}{r} 4 \\ + 9 \\ \hline \end{array}$$

5.
$$\begin{array}{r} 10 \\ + 7 \\ \hline \end{array}$$

8.
$$\begin{array}{r} 8 \\ + 8 \\ \hline \end{array}$$

3.
$$\begin{array}{r} 18 \\ + 0 \\ \hline \end{array}$$

6.
$$\begin{array}{r} 12 \\ + 3 \\ \hline \end{array}$$

9.
$$\begin{array}{r} 5 \\ + 9 \\ \hline \end{array}$$

4.
$$\begin{array}{r} 7 \\ + 8 \\ \hline \end{array}$$

7.
$$\begin{array}{r} 13 \\ + 3 \\ \hline \end{array}$$

10.
$$\begin{array}{r} 11 \\ + 5 \\ \hline \end{array}$$

Answer the questions.

11. What is the highest number you can roll with 3 number cubes?

_____

12. What is the lowest number you can roll with 3 number cubes?

_____

Name _____

Draw a picture. Mark off to subtract.

1. Ten children were playing in a pool. Five got out. How many children are still in the pool?

10	😊🙂😊🙂😊
− 5	🚫🚫🚫🚫🚫

____ children

2.
```
  10
−  3
```

5.
```
   9
−  7
```

7.
```
  12
−  6
```

3.
```
  13
−  4
```

8.
```
  11
−  2
```

4.
```
  12
−  9
```

6.
```
  16
−  8
```

9.
```
  18
−  9
```

Solve.

10.

 − 5 cents = _____ ¢

11.

 − 3 cents = _____ ¢

12.

 − 5 cents = _____ ¢

If the answer is correct, circle it. If the answer is incorrect, mark it off and write the correct answer.

13.
$$\begin{array}{r} 12 \\ -\ 9 \\ \hline 4 \end{array}$$

15.
$$\begin{array}{r} 11 \\ -\ 8 \\ \hline 3 \end{array}$$

17.
$$\begin{array}{r} 12 \\ -\ 4 \\ \hline 8 \end{array}$$

14.
$$\begin{array}{r} 11 \\ -\ 4 \\ \hline 6 \end{array}$$

16.
$$\begin{array}{r} 10 \\ -\ 8 \\ \hline 3 \end{array}$$

18.
$$\begin{array}{r} 14 \\ -\ 6 \\ \hline 6 \end{array}$$

Read and answer the question. Draw the children now skating on the pond.

19. There were 15 children skating on a pond. Then, 7 went home. How many children stayed at the pond?

_____ children

Use a calculator to solve the exercises in one section. Do not use a calculator for the other section.

1.
$$83 - 42$$

3.
$$67 + 10$$

5.
$$86 + 12$$

2.
$$41 + 25$$

4.
$$88 - 44$$

6.
$$25 - 13$$

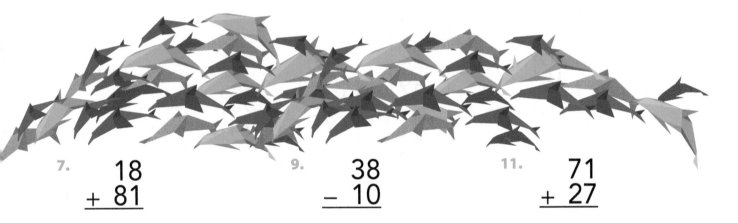

7.
$$18 + 81$$

9.
$$38 - 10$$

11.
$$71 + 27$$

8.
$$82 - 51$$

10.
$$26 + 31$$

12.
$$67 - 56$$

13. Use a calculator to check the sum in each box.
If the answer is correct, color the box.
Follow the colored boxes to find what
Kay will catch.

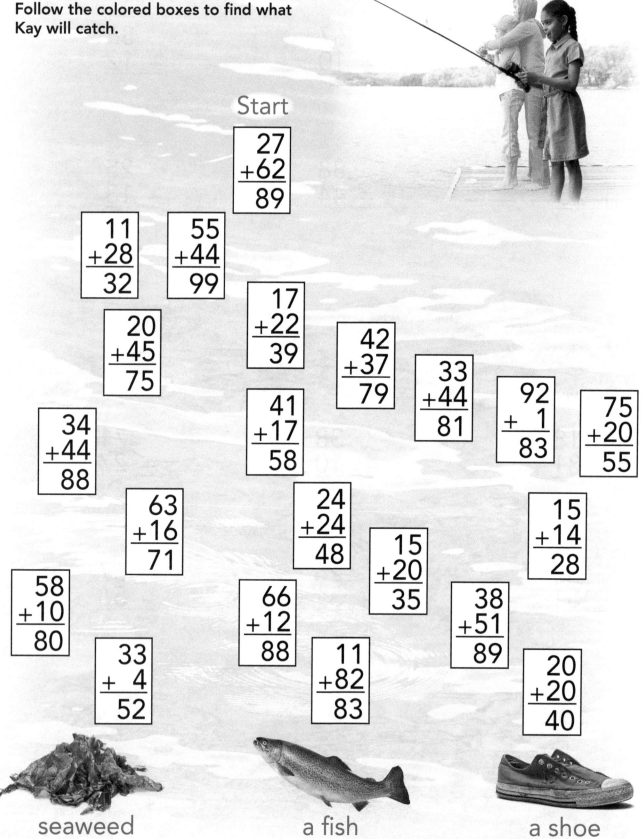

Start

```
  27
 +62
 ───
  89
```

```
  11
 +28
 ───
  32
```

```
  55
 +44
 ───
  99
```

```
  20
 +45
 ───
  75
```

```
  17
 +22
 ───
  39
```

```
  42
 +37
 ───
  79
```

```
  33
 +44
 ───
  81
```

```
  92
 + 1
 ───
  83
```

```
  75
 +20
 ───
  55
```

```
  34
 +44
 ───
  88
```

```
  41
 +17
 ───
  58
```

```
  63
 +16
 ───
  71
```

```
  24
 +24
 ───
  48
```

```
  15
 +20
 ───
  35
```

```
  15
 +14
 ───
  28
```

```
  58
 +10
 ───
  80
```

```
  66
 +12
 ───
  88
```

```
  38
 +51
 ───
  89
```

```
  33
 + 4
 ───
  52
```

```
  11
 +82
 ───
  83
```

```
  20
 +20
 ───
  40
```

seaweed   a fish   a shoe

258 two hundred fifty-eight

Count the items. Draw in the blank ten-frames. Find the sums.

1.
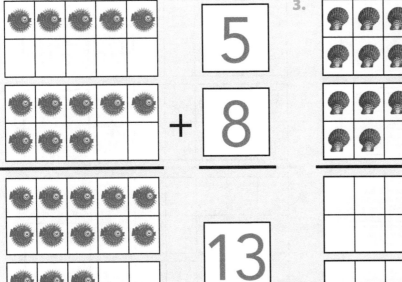

5

$+$

8

13

2.

$+$

3.

$+$

4.

$+$

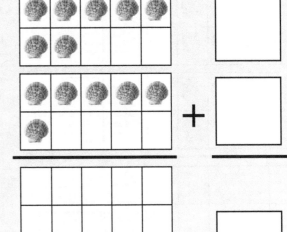

Count the doubles. Draw in the blank ten-frames. Find the sums.

5.

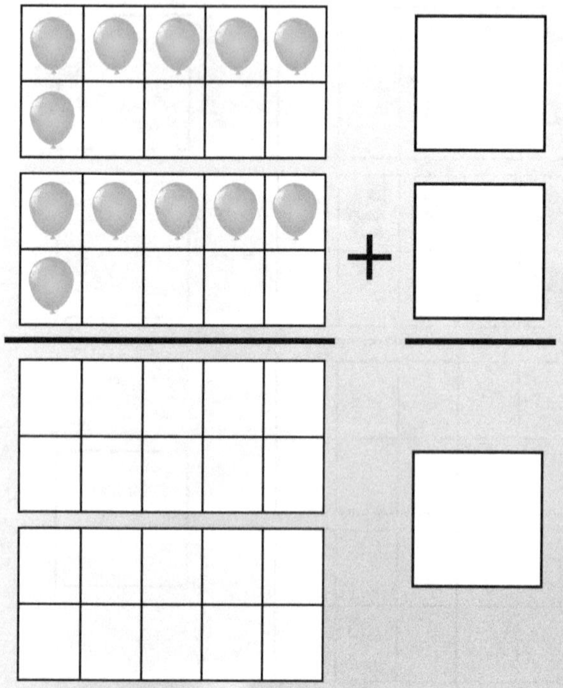

+

7.

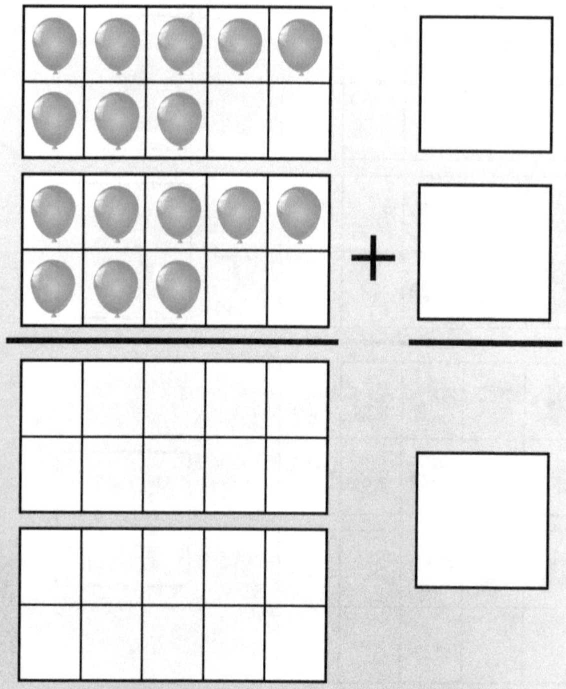

+

6.

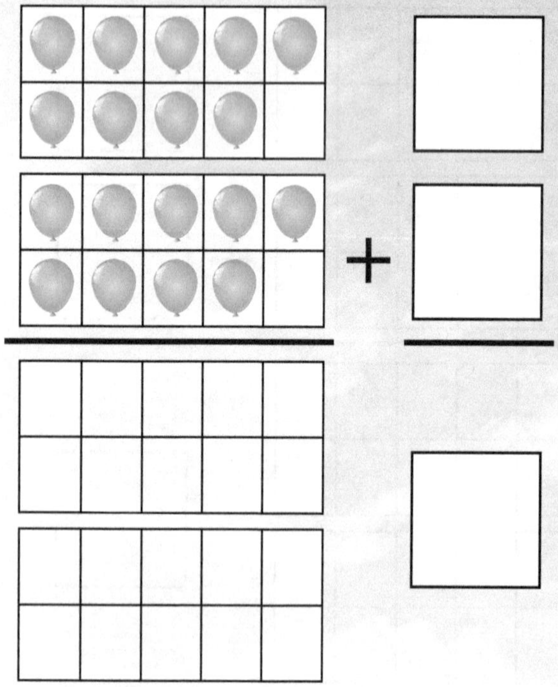

+

8.

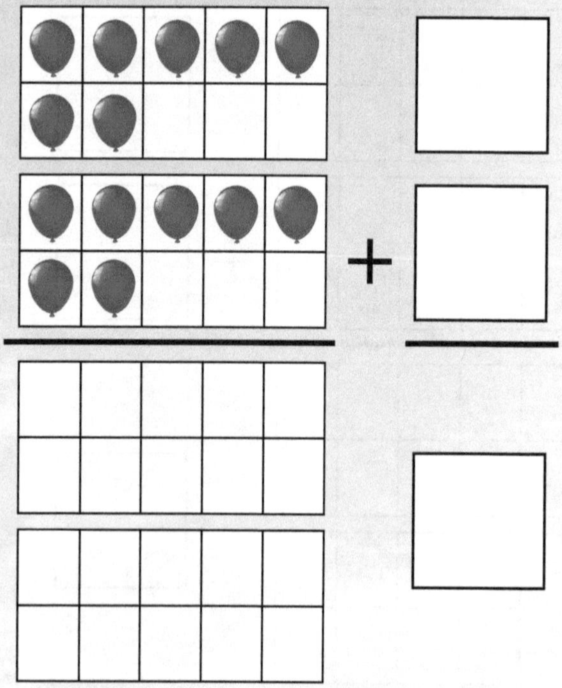

+

Name _____

Mark off to subtract. Find the differences.

1.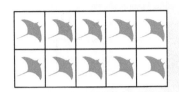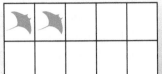

$- 8$

2.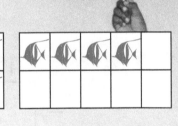

$- 5$

3.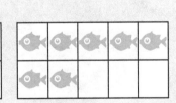

$- 9$

Roll a number cube. Write the number rolled. Subtract.

4.
$$
\begin{array}{r}
16 \\
- \ \square \\
\hline
\end{array}
$$

7.
$$
\begin{array}{r}
13 \\
- \ \square \\
\hline
\end{array}
$$

10.
$$
\begin{array}{r}
8 \\
- \ \square \\
\hline
\end{array}
$$

5.
$$
\begin{array}{r}
11 \\
- \ \square \\
\hline
\end{array}
$$

8.
$$
\begin{array}{r}
14 \\
- \ \square \\
\hline
\end{array}
$$

11.
$$
\begin{array}{r}
12 \\
- \ \square \\
\hline
\end{array}
$$

6.
$$
\begin{array}{r}
6 \\
- \ \square \\
\hline
\end{array}
$$

9.
$$
\begin{array}{r}
15 \\
- \ \square \\
\hline
\end{array}
$$

12.
$$
\begin{array}{r}
10 \\
- \ \square \\
\hline
\end{array}
$$

Read and answer the question.

13. During a fishing contest, three children caught 18 fish. The children threw 7 fish back into the water. How many were kept?

_____ fish

Name _____

Add with Base 10 Blocks 9.6

Add.

1.

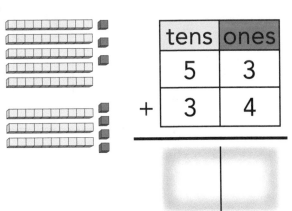

	tens	ones
	5	3
+	3	4

3.

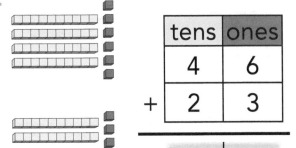

	tens	ones
	4	6
+	2	3

2.

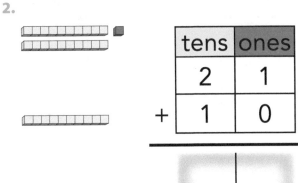

	tens	ones
	2	1
+	1	0

4.

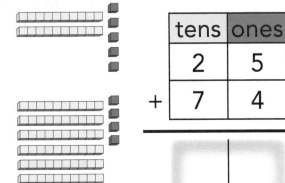

	tens	ones
	2	5
+	7	4

5. Circle the dimes and pennies needed to make the same number shown with the Base 10 blocks.

Write the number. _____

© *Mathematics* Grade 1

Write the problems. Solve.

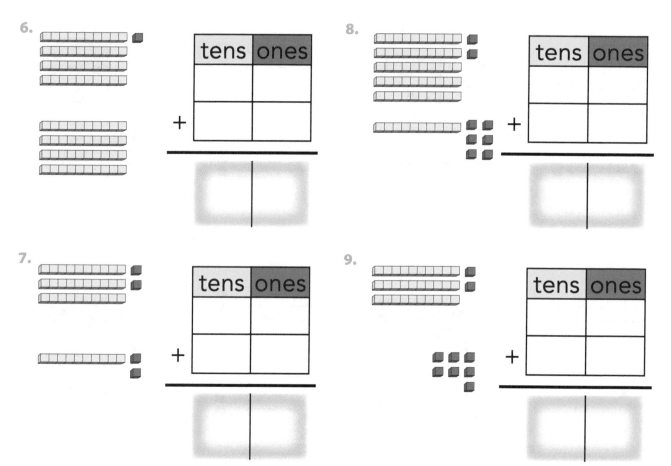

6.

tens	ones
+	

8.

tens	ones
+	

7.

tens	ones
+	

9.

tens	ones
+	

Find the values.

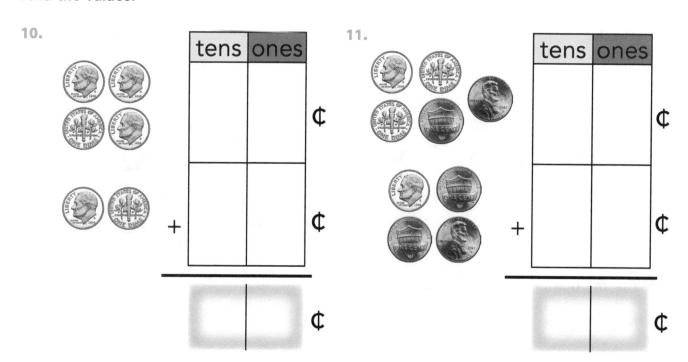

10.

tens	ones
		¢
+		¢
		¢

11.

tens	ones
		¢
+		¢
		¢

264 two hundred sixty-four

Fill in the boxes. Mark off to subtract. Solve. Write the differences.

1. Start with 34.
   Subtract 11.

   You have _____.

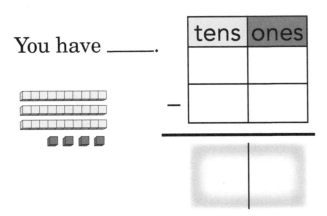

4. Start with 57.
   Subtract 45.

   You have _____.

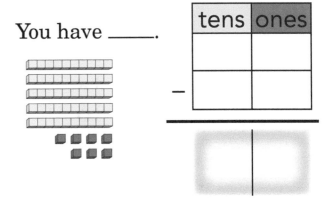

2. Start with 95.
   Subtract 61.

   You have _____.

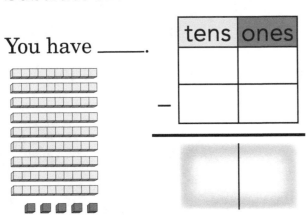

5. Start with 18.
   Subtract 13.

   You have _____.

3. Start with 80.
   Subtract 40.

   You have _____.

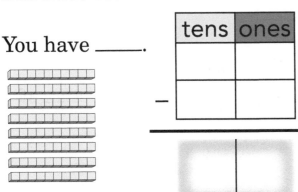

6. Start with 26.
   Subtract 6.

   You have _____.

Write the differences.

7.
$$\begin{array}{r} 45 \\ - 34 \\ \hline \end{array}$$

9.
$$\begin{array}{r} 77 \\ - 51 \\ \hline \end{array}$$

11.
$$\begin{array}{r} 23 \\ - 12 \\ \hline \end{array}$$

13.
$$\begin{array}{r} 47 \\ - 24 \\ \hline \end{array}$$

8.
$$\begin{array}{r} 90 \\ - 10 \\ \hline \end{array}$$

10.
$$\begin{array}{r} 18 \\ - 16 \\ \hline \end{array}$$

12.
$$\begin{array}{r} 39 \\ - 28 \\ \hline \end{array}$$

14.
$$\begin{array}{r} 86 \\ - 56 \\ \hline \end{array}$$

Read and answer the question. Solve.

15. Miguel had   .

He bought a red ribbon for 11¢. How much does he have left?

_____ ¢

Review

16. Count the money.

      = _____ ¢

Add with Tens Mats 9.8

Draw cups and beans on the blank workmats. Write the numbers. Add.

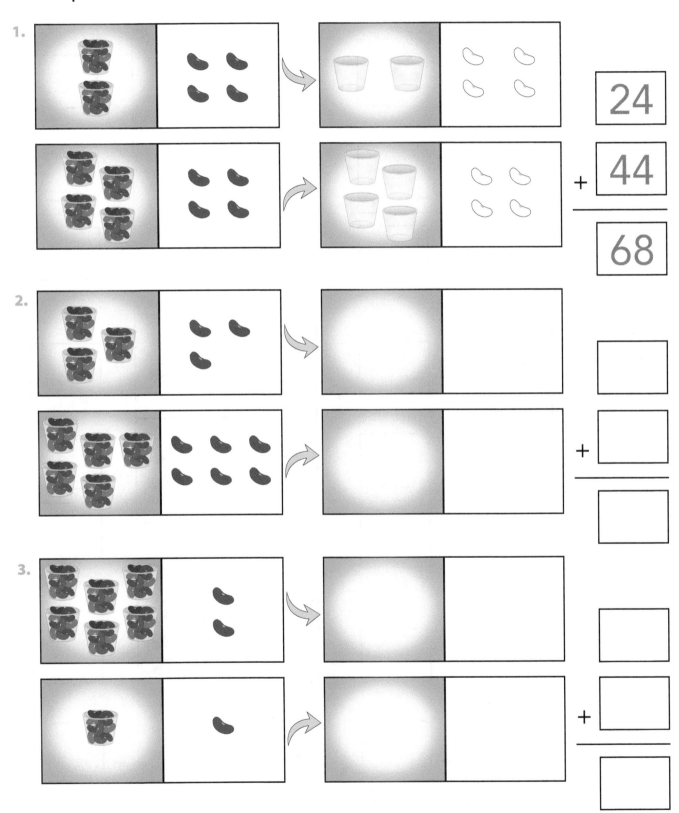

Write the numbers. Find the sums.

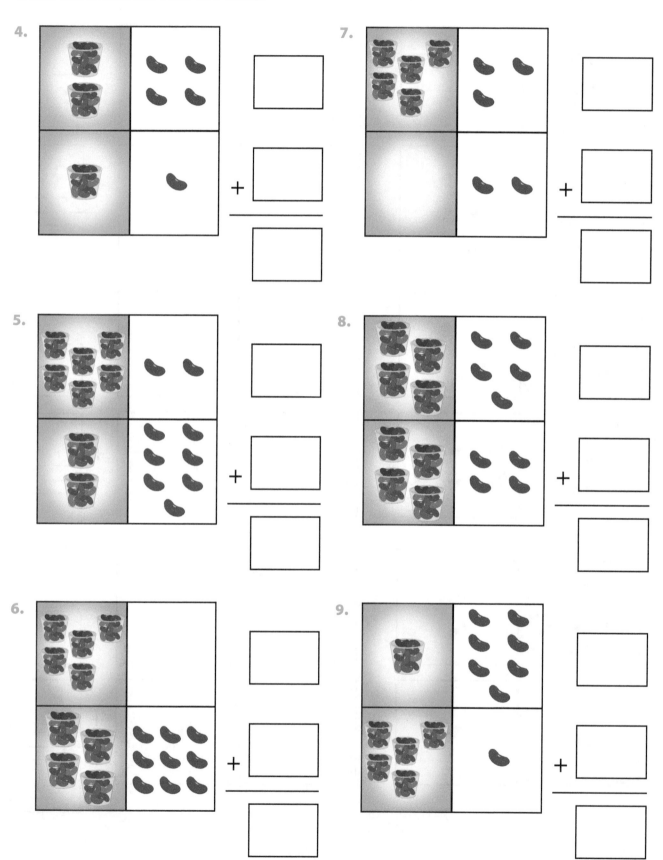

4.

□
+
□
―――
□

7.

□
+
□
―――
□

5.

□
+
□
―――
□

8.

□
+
□
―――
□

6.

□
+
□
―――
□

9.

□
+
□
―――
□

Mark off to subtract.

1.
$$64 - 20$$
[   ]
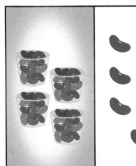

4.
$$47 - 13$$
[   ]

2.
$$49 - 16$$
[   ]
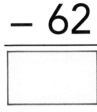

5.
$$87 - 62$$
[   ]

3.
$$25 - 25$$
[   ]
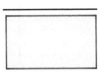 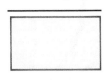

6.
$$53 - 41$$
[   ]

Write subtraction problems of your own.

7.
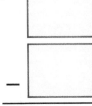

8.

Write the differences. Subtract the ones first.

9.
tens	ones
2	4
−	3
2	1

11.
tens	ones
7	9
− 4	6

13.
tens	ones
5	5
− 5	2

15.
tens	ones
6	6
− 5	2

10.
tens	ones
4	8
− 2	6

12.
tens	ones
8	9
− 4	2

14.
tens	ones
3	5
− 1	5

16.
tens	ones
2	7
− 1	4

17. **Color the answers from above** green. **Color all other numbers** blue.

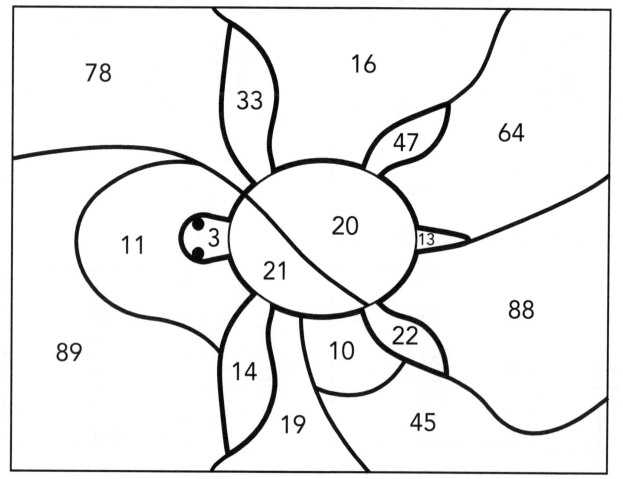

Color the blocks needed to match the number.

1.

452

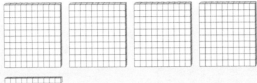

2.

736

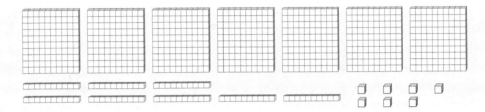

3.

234

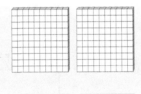

4.

866

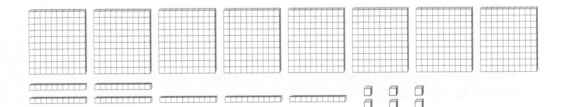

Add the ones first.

Add the tens next.

Add the hundreds last.

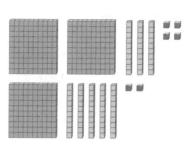

hundreds	tens	ones
2	3	4
+ 1	5	2
3	8	6

Add.

5.

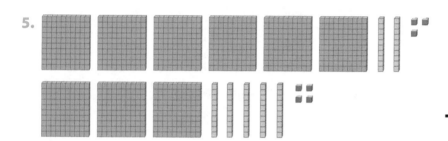

hundreds	tens	ones
+		

6.

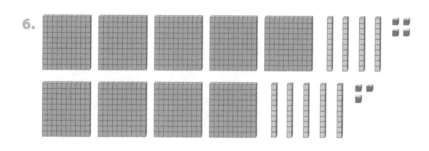

hundreds	tens	ones
+		

Review

Solve.

7.
$$\begin{array}{r} 7 \\ + 7 \\ \hline \end{array}$$

8.
$$\begin{array}{r} 8 \\ + 3 \\ \hline \end{array}$$

9.
$$\begin{array}{r} 2 \\ + 7 \\ \hline \end{array}$$

10.
$$\begin{array}{r} 9 \\ + 7 \\ \hline \end{array}$$

11.
$$\begin{array}{r} 6 \\ + 6 \\ \hline \end{array}$$

12. $5 + 2 + 6 = $ _____

13. $1 + 7 + 3 = $ _____

Read and circle the answer.

1. Annie wrote this problem on her whiteboard:

$$\begin{array}{r} 7\ 1 \\ +\ 7\ 1 \\ \hline 8\ 2 \end{array}$$

Is the answer right?

yes   no

Draw a line between the tens and ones. Add the ones first. Write the sums.

2.
$$\begin{array}{r} 48 \\ +\ 51 \\ \hline \end{array}$$

3.
$$\begin{array}{r} 70 \\ +\ \ 5 \\ \hline \end{array}$$

4.
$$\begin{array}{r} 80 \\ +\ 13 \\ \hline \end{array}$$

5.
$$\begin{array}{r} 47 \\ +\ 10 \\ \hline \end{array}$$

6.
$$\begin{array}{r} 94 \\ +\ \ 2 \\ \hline \end{array}$$

7. Write the sums above in order from the least to the greatest.

_____   _____   _____   _____   _____

8. Use a calculator. Add the two greatest sums.

[ ] + [ ] = [ ]

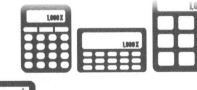

Draw a line between the hundreds, tens, and ones. Add the ones first. Write the sums.

9. 120
    + 29

11. 33
    +16

13. 324
    + 15

15. 521
    +344

10. 125
    + 22

12. 106
    + 31

14. 220
    + 18

16. 144
    + 12

Write the missing addends. Use the numbers on the fish.

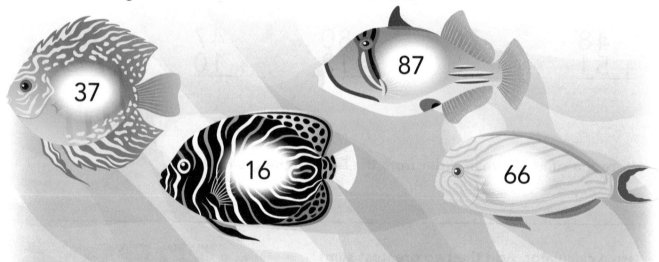

37

87

16

66

17. 83
    + ☐
    ___
     99

18. 62
    + ☐
    ___
     99

19. 33
    + ☐
    ___
     99

20. 12
    + ☐
    ___
     99

Name _____

Subtract. Begin with the ones.

1.

hundreds	tens	ones
5	6	5
− 1	3	2

3.

hundreds	tens	ones
4	5	7
−	2	3

2.

hundreds	tens	ones
2	6	4
− 2	0	3

4.

hundreds	tens	ones
6	9	9
− 2	7	5

5. Write the differences above in order from greatest to least.

_____ _____ _____ _____

6. Two of the answers have a difference of 1. Write the number sentence.

 − =

Shawn's Shell Shop

Write the subtraction problems. Solve.

7.
69¢   69¢
−   −   ¢
                ¢

8.
26¢   26¢
−   −   ¢
                ¢

9.
98¢   98¢
−   −   ¢
                ¢

10.
39¢   39¢
−   −   ¢
                ¢

Review

Measure these lines in inches.

11. ⊢————————————⊣ ____ inches

12. ⊢———————————⊣ ____ inches

Write the problem in the space provided. Write + or −. Solve.

1. Wendy and Ricardo found 77 shells at the beach. They used 30 shells to decorate a sand castle. How many shells are left?

tens	ones

_____ shells

2. Suki's teacher needs 56 beads for art. Suki counted 29 blue beads. She counted 30 green ones. Will there be enough beads?

tens	ones

yes   no

3. Mando caught a 244-pound shark. He caught a 20-pound tuna. How many pounds of fish did he catch in all?

hundreds	tens	ones

_____ pounds

Write the problem in the space provided. Write + or −. Solve.

4. Emet put 65 cents into the offering.
Then he found 3 dimes and 2 pennies.
He put those into the offering too.
How much money did Emet give?

_____ cents

dimes	pennies

5. Riya saw some coins on the sidewalk.
She picked up 1 dime and 7 pennies.
Then she found 2 dimes and 2 pennies.
How many cents did Riya find in all?

_____ cents

dimes	pennies

6. Tan's mom gave him $1.99 to spend.
Tan spent 1 dollar and 45 cents. How
much money did Tan have left?

_____ cents

dollars	dimes	pennies

Review

Measure these lines in centimeters.

7. ├────────────────────────┤   _____ centimeters

8. ├──────────────────┤   _____ centimeters

Solve. Match the answer to the picture.

1. 24
  + 31
  [ ]

2. 59
  − 47
  [ ]

3. 66
  + 12
  [ ]

4. 83
  − 23
  [ ]

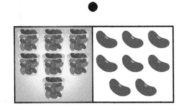
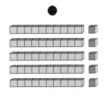

60

Read and match.

5. Julie rolled 3 number cubes. She wrote the numbers.

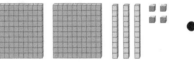   • 623

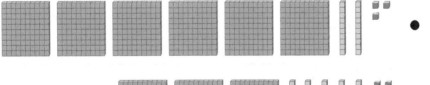   • 234

          • 453

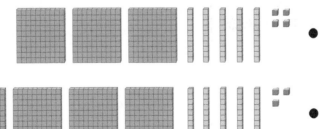   • 354

Roll two number cubes. Write the numbers. Mark off to subtract.

6.
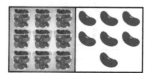

| 9 | 7 |

−
| | |

| | |

7.
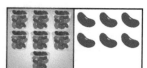

| 7 | 6 |

−
| | |

| | |

Solve.

8.
$$214 \atop +154$$

10.
$$442 \atop +117$$

12.
$$79 \atop -\ 30$$

14.
$$742 \atop -512$$

9.
$$14 \atop +\ 54$$

11.
$$93 \atop -\ 72$$

13.
$$386 \atop -133$$

15.
$$58 \atop -\ 57$$

Read and answer the question. Draw a picture.

16. Soo sees 6 crabs walking on the sand. Each crab has 6 legs. How many legs are there altogether?

_____ legs

Write the greater than > or less than < sign.

1. 25 ◯ 47

2. 37 ◯ 73

3. 61 ◯ 19

4. 24 ◯ 42

Color the shape or set to match the fraction.

5. $\frac{3}{4}$

6. $\frac{2}{3}$

7. $\frac{1}{2}$

8. $\frac{1}{4}$

Write the number of tens and ones. Add.

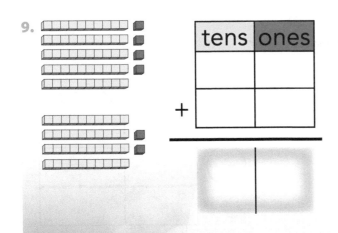

9.

tens	ones
+	

10.

tens	ones
+	

Solve.

11.
$$\begin{array}{r} 24 \\ + 31 \\ \hline \end{array}$$

13.
$$\begin{array}{r} 59 \\ - 47 \\ \hline \end{array}$$

15.
$$\begin{array}{r} 766 \\ +112 \\ \hline \end{array}$$

17.
$$\begin{array}{r} 483 \\ -123 \\ \hline \end{array}$$

12.
$$\begin{array}{r} 545 \\ - 34 \\ \hline \end{array}$$

14.
$$\begin{array}{r} 677 \\ -351 \\ \hline \end{array}$$

16.
$$\begin{array}{r} 23 \\ - 12 \\ \hline \end{array}$$

18.
$$\begin{array}{r} 39 \\ - 28 \\ \hline \end{array}$$

Write the number.

19. = _____

20. 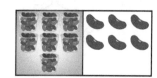 = _____

Read the word problem. Fill in the numbers and write + or −. Solve.

21. Alma had 6 dimes and 3 pennies. Then she lost 21 cents. How much money does she have now?

_____ cents

dimes	pennies

◯

Circle the coins to show how much money Alma has now.

22.

Chapter 10
Graphs and Maps

If I go up to the heavens, You are there; if I make my bed in the depths, You are there. If I rise on the wings of the dawn, if I settle on the far side of the sea, even there Your hand will guide me, Your right hand will hold me fast.
Psalm 139:8–10

Key Ideas:

Probability and Statistics: collecting and organizing data

Probability and Statistics: making and interpreting tables, pictographs, and bar graphs

Algebra: using ordered pairs

Read the bar graph. Color the same number of spots on the turtle.

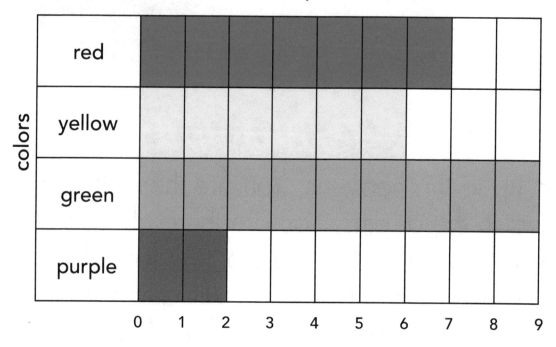

A Venn diagram is a picture. It uses circles to show how sets are alike or different.

1. Circle the shells that would go in the middle section.

These are Jada's shells.

These are Justin's shells.

2. Write the letters in the correct circle.

P X S

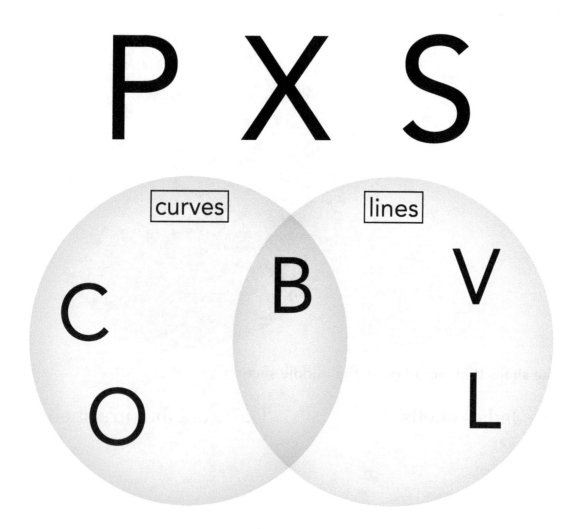

3. Write A, B, or M for middle to show where each object should go.

A graph is a chart that shows information. Here are some kinds of graphs.

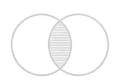 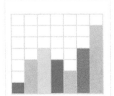  

1. Look at the pictures. Write the letters on the Venn diagram.

blue   both blue and orange   orange

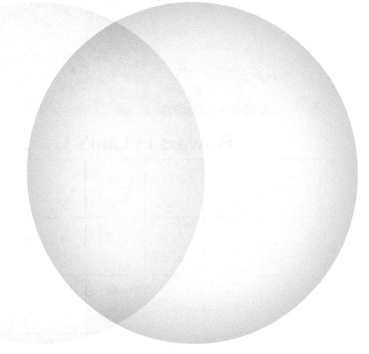

A

B

C

D

E

F

2. Color one flower on the graph for each flower in the picture. Answer the questions.

Flowers in Lani's Garden

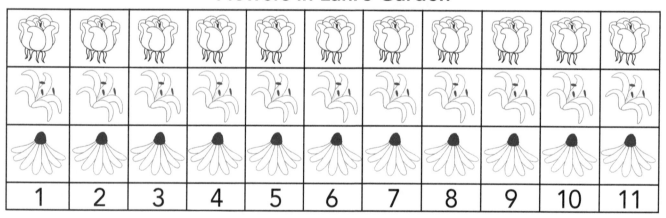

3. How many 🌹? _____

4. How many 🌿? _____

5. How many 🌼? _____

This pictograph shows the number of little clocks that each teacher has. Look at the key. Answer the questions.

Student Clocks

Miss Moreno	🕐 🕐 🕐 🕐 🕐
Mr. Connor	🕐 🕐 🕐
Mrs. Patil	🕐 🕐 🕐 🕐 🕐 🕐 🕐

key
🕐 = 5 clocks

1. Miss Moreno has 20 students in her class. She wants them all to have clocks. How many clocks does she have?

   _____ clocks

2. Does Miss Moreno have enough clocks?   yes   or   no

3. Does she have any left over?   yes   or   no

4. How many clocks does Mr. Connor have? _____ clocks

5. Who has more clocks than Miss Moreno? _____

6. Mrs. Patil wants 20 more clocks. Can she borrow enough from Mr. Connor?

   yes   or   no

Read the pictograph. Answer the questions.

Ships Served by Lighthouses

🚢	West Quoddy Head	🚢 🚢 🚢 🚢 🚢
🚢	Peggy's Cove	🚢 🚢 🚢
🚢	Portland Head	🚢 🚢 🚢 🚢 🚢 🚢
🚢	Tybee Island	🚢 🚢 🚢 🚢

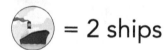 = 2 ships

7. Which lighthouse served 8 ships?

_____

8. How many ships sailed by the Portland Head lighthouse?

_____ ships

9. How many more ships sailed by the West Quoddy Head lighthouse than the Tybee Island lighthouse?

_____ ships   _____ – _____ = _____

10. How many ships were served by the West Quoddy Head lighthouse and the Peggy's Cove lighthouse altogether?

_____ ships   _____ + _____ = _____

11. How many ships were served altogether? _____ ships

Bears

color of bears

1. Color a bar graph to match the pictograph.

Bears

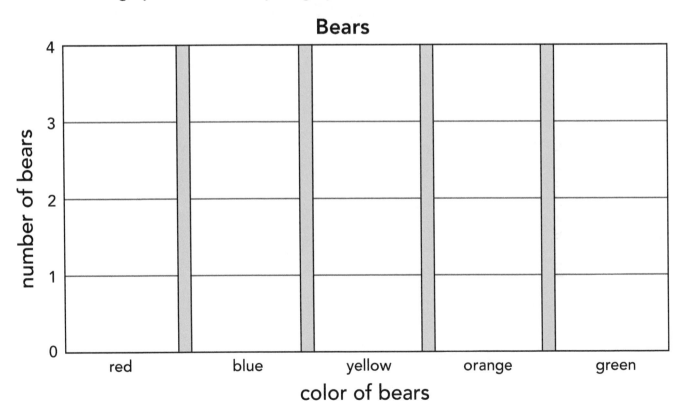

Mr. Garcia's students had a vote. They voted for their favorite kind of ice cream. They made a table.

2. Read the table. Make tallies for the votes. Color the bar graph to match the numbers in the table. Start coloring the graph from the bottom.

Ice Cream Flavors

	votes	tallies
chocolate	9	
vanilla	7	
strawberry	6	

Ice Cream Flavors

What is in the sea? There are plants, fish, shells, and boats. What are some things you have seen?

1. Cut out the pictures. Sort them into sets. Glue them in place to make a graph.

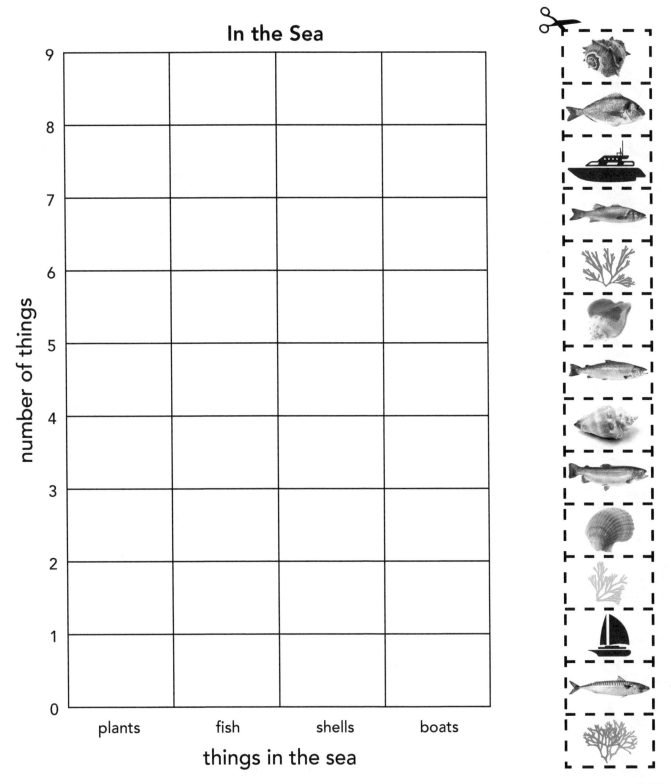

2. Count the fish. Color rectangles to make a bar graph. Write a title.

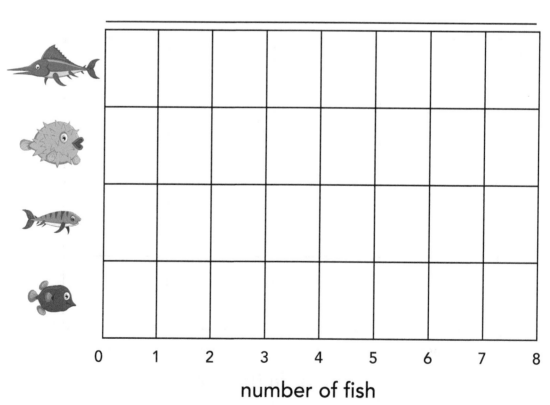

number of fish

Follow the directions. Use the boat and sail you have been given.

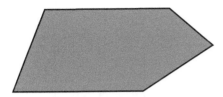

Cut out your boat.

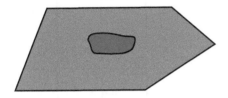

Set a piece of play dough in the middle of the boat.

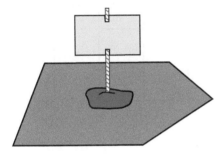

Put a sail on the straw.
Then, place the straw in the play dough.

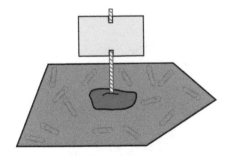

Place sailors on your boat.
Put as many sailors on your boat as you can.
Do not let the sailors touch each other.

Sailors can be pennies, paper clips, beans, and macaroni.

1. Count the sailors. Make a table to match your boat.

My Boat

sailors	tallies	number
pennies		
paper clips		
beans		
macaroni		

2. Make a graph of your boat. Write a title.

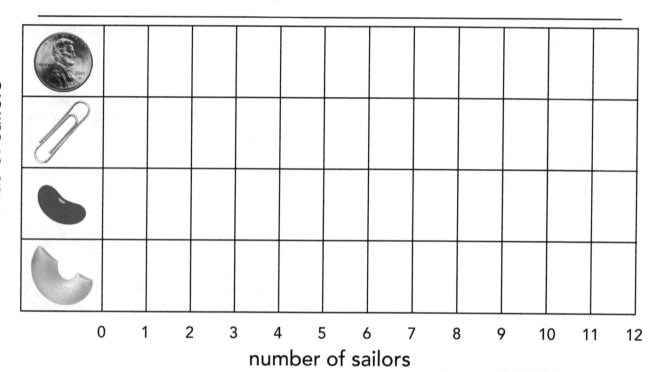

kinds of sailors

0   1   2   3   4   5   6   7   8   9   10   11   12

number of sailors

Complete the sentences.

3. My boat carried _____ sailors in all.

4. I had _____ pennies.

5. I had _____ paper clips.

6. I had _____ beans.

7. I had _____ macaroni.

8. I had the most _____ and the least _____.

9. What is the difference between the greatest and the least? Write

a number sentence. _____

Lighthouses

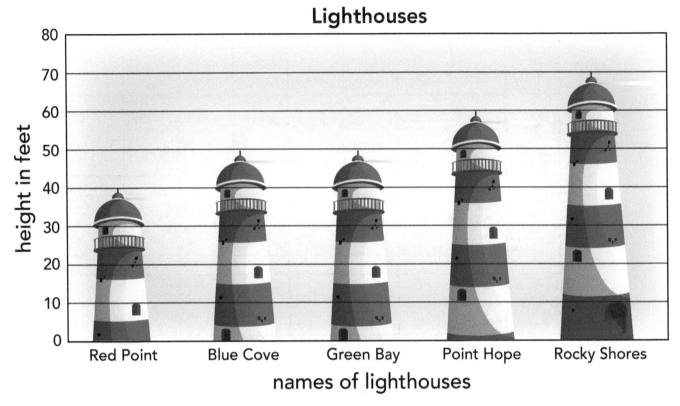

height in feet

Red Point   Blue Cove   Green Bay   Point Hope   Rocky Shores

names of lighthouses

Use the graph to solve the word problems.

1. How tall is the tallest lighthouse? _____ feet

2. How tall is the shortest lighthouse? _____ feet

Solve. Show your work.

3. How much taller is the Rocky Shores
   lighthouse than the Red Point lighthouse?

   _____ feet

tens	ones
−

4. If the Green Bay lighthouse were placed
   on top of the Red Point lighthouse, how
   tall would they be altogether?

   _____ feet

tens	ones
+

Popcorn

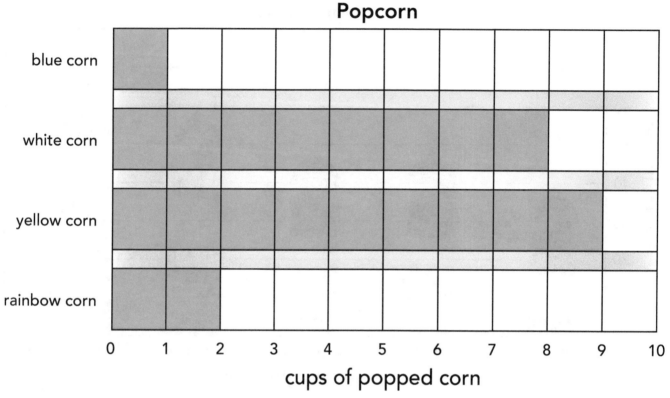

cups of popped corn

Use the graph to solve the word problems.

Shelly and her friend Tony popped four kinds of popcorn. The graph shows how many cups of popped corn they had after popping.

5. Which popcorn had the greatest number of cups? _____

6. Which popcorn had the least number of cups? _____

7. How many cups of white popcorn were there? _____ cups

8. What is the difference in number between the blue popcorn and

the yellow popcorn? _____ cups

Area is the number of square units that cover a surface.

Count the square inches to find the area of each shape.

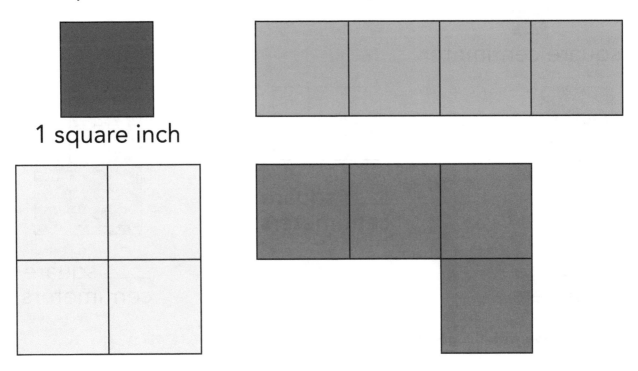

1 square inch

Each shape is different but all have the same area, 4 square inches.

What is the area of each shape below? Write the number of square inches.

1.

2.

_____ square inches

3.

_____ square inches

_____ square inches

Each shape is made of square centimeters. What is the area of each shape? Write the number of square centimeters.

1 square centimeter

4.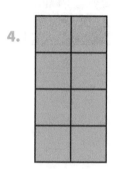

_____ square centimeters

5.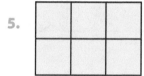

_____ square centimeters

6.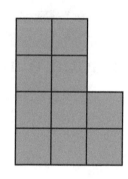

_____ square centimeters

Circle the shape with the greater area.

7. 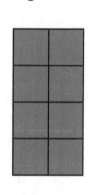 or

8. 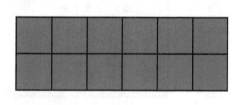 or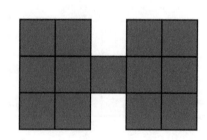

9. 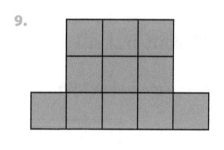 or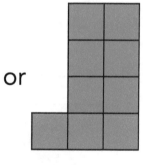

Name _____

Hannah and Ethan's Canoe

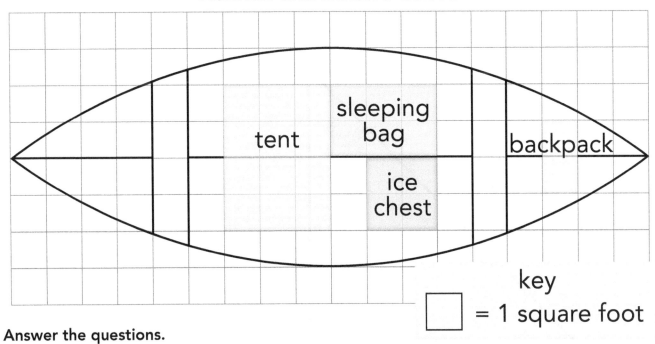

key
☐ = 1 square foot

Answer the questions.

1. Hannah and Ethan are going on a canoe trip with their parents. How much area in the bottom of the canoe is covered by the tent?

   _____ square feet

2. By the sleeping bag? _____ square feet

3. By the backpack? _____ square feet

4. By the ice chest? _____ square feet

5. Is the area of the canoe greater than or less than 50 square feet? Circle your answer.

   greater than   less than

6. Find the area of the sail. Color the whole squares of the sail one color. Color the half squares another color. Count 2 half squares as 1 whole square. Tally your counts.

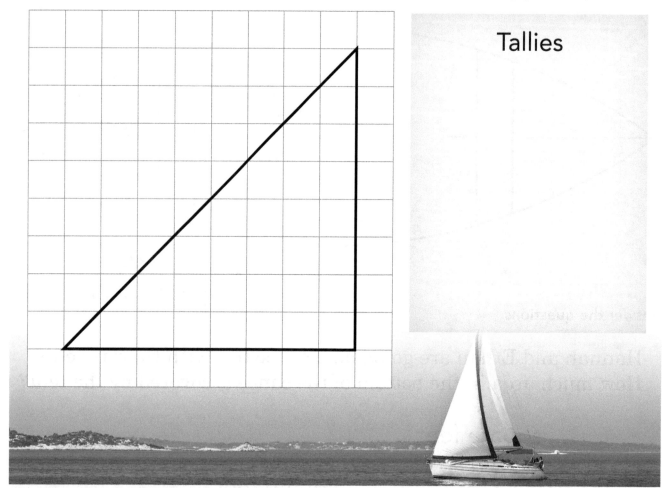

Tallies

Review

Add or subtract.

7.
$$\begin{array}{r} 8 \\ + \ 3 \\ \hline \end{array}$$

9.
$$\begin{array}{r} 31 \\ - \ 20 \\ \hline \end{array}$$

11.
$$\begin{array}{r} 16 \\ + \ 42 \\ \hline \end{array}$$

13.
$$\begin{array}{r} 7 \\ + \ 5 \\ \hline \end{array}$$

8.
$$\begin{array}{r} 86 \\ - \ 46 \\ \hline \end{array}$$

10.
$$\begin{array}{r} 71 \\ + \ 15 \\ \hline \end{array}$$

12.
$$\begin{array}{r} 53 \\ + \ 33 \\ \hline \end{array}$$

14.
$$\begin{array}{r} 12 \\ - \ 5 \\ \hline \end{array}$$

Lighthouses in North America

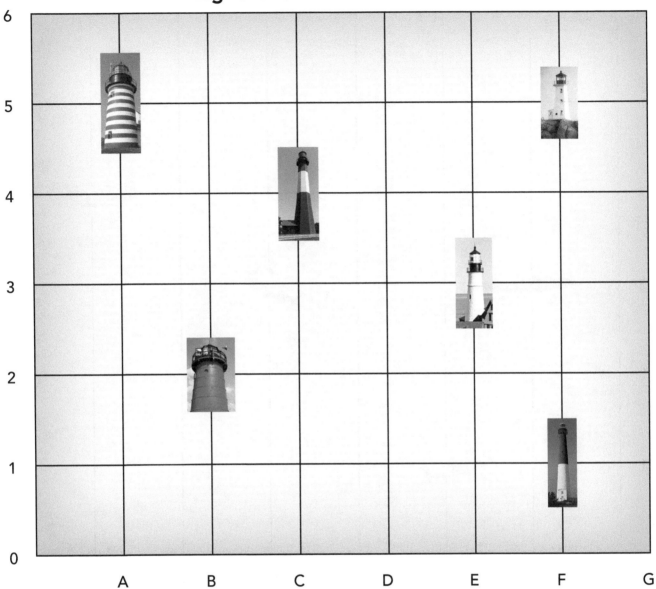

Follow the directions to find each lighthouse. Circle the correct lighthouse.

1. **B2**   Go ⟶ to B. Go ↑ to 2.   or

2. **E3**   Go ⟶ to E. Go ↑ to 3.   or

3. **F5**   Go ⟶ to F. Go ↑ to 5.   or

4. **C4**   Go ⟶ to C. Go ↑ to 4.   or

Boat Float

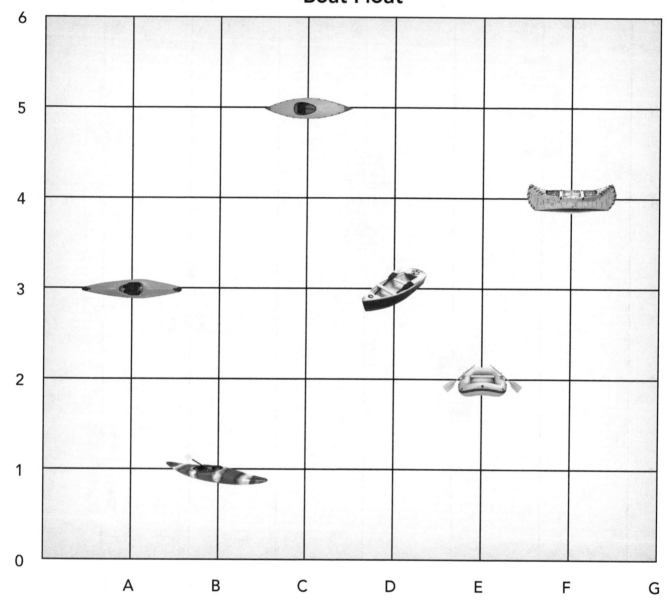

Follow the directions to find each boat. Circle the correct boat.

5. **C5**   Go ⟶ to C. Go ↑ to 5.      or   [boat image]

6. **F4**   Go ⟶ to F. Go ↑ to 4.      or   [boat image]

7. **B1**   Go ⟶ to B. Go ↑ to 1.      or   [boat image]

8. **A3**   Go ⟶ to A. Go ↑ to 3.      or   [boat image]

My Neighborhood

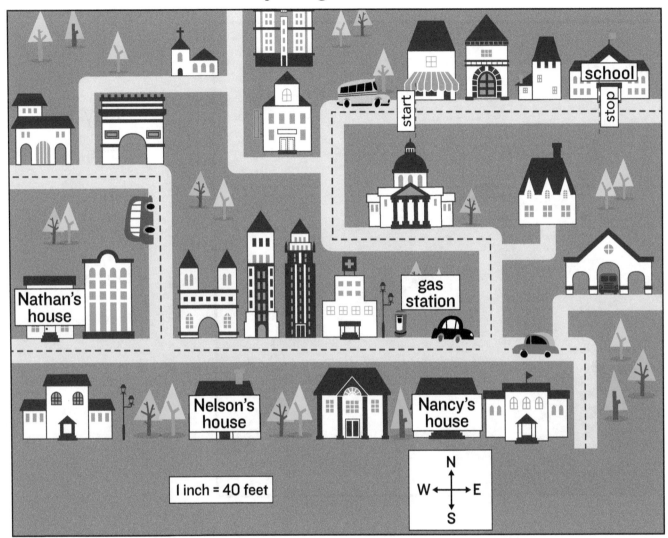

I inch = 40 feet

Look at the map. Follow the directions.

1. Write the title of the map. _____

2. Circle the compass rose. Draw a rectangle around the scale.

3. How many feet does the bus have to drive to get to the school?

   _____ + _____ = _____ feet

4. Is Nancy's house east or west of Nelson's house? _____

5. Is the gas station north or south of the bus? _____

Look at the map below. Read the map key and the sentences. Circle yes or no.

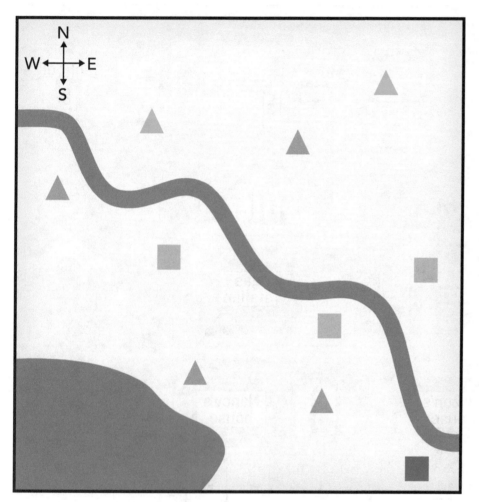

key

■ = office

■ = cabin

▲ = small tent site

▲ = big tent site

6. There are four big tent sites.   **yes**   or   **no**

7. There are two big tent sites.   **yes**   or   **no**

8. Cabins are on both sides of the river.   **yes**   or   **no**

9. The office is west of the pond.   **yes**   or   **no**

10. The big tent sites are north of the river.   **yes**   or   **no**

11. The pond is south of the cabins.   **yes**   or   **no**

12. Choose a cabin or tent site. Label it "My Spot."

Look at the map and the map key. Read and follow the directions.

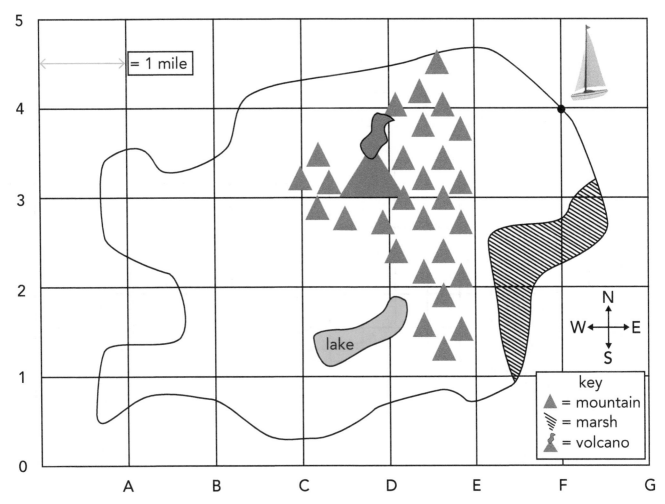

1. Start at the sailboat.
2. Go west 1 mile.
3. Go south 3 miles.
4. Go west 2 miles.
5. Go north 1 mile.
6. Go east 1 mile. Mark that spot with an X for buried treasure.

7. Write the letter and number that tells where the treasure is

buried. _____

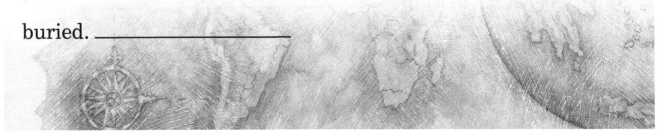

This is a map of the playground. Look at the compass rose. Answer the questions.

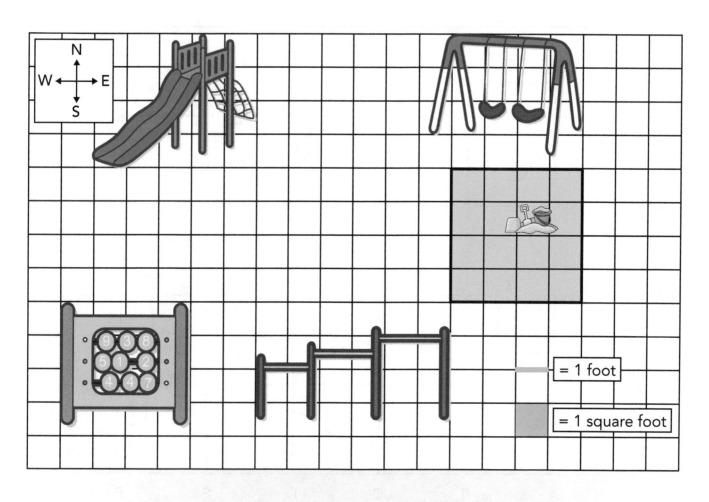

8. What is the area of the sandbox? _____ square feet

9. What is the length of all the pull-up bars? _____ feet

10. How far is the green number board from the pull-up bars?

    _____ feet

11. What is east of the slide? _____

12. What is south of the swing set? _____

Name _____

The first graders at Grace Christian School brought toys to school. The toys were for children in poor countries. The graph shows the number of toys the students brought each day.

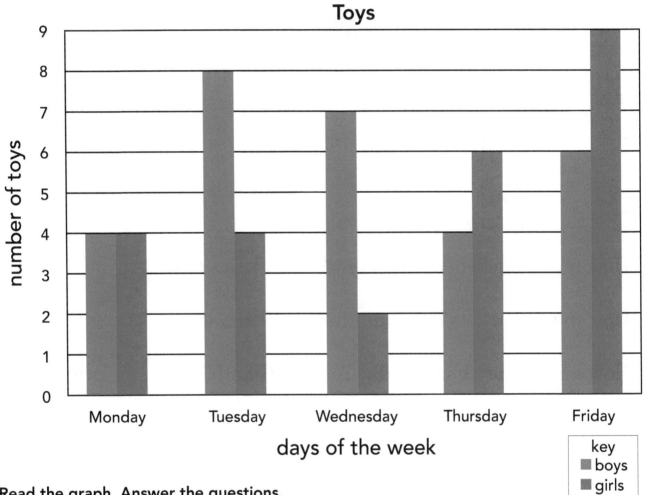

Toys

number of toys / days of the week

key
■ boys
■ girls

Read the graph. Answer the questions.

1. How many toys did the boys bring on Tuesday? _____ toys

2. Did the boys or girls bring more toys on Friday? _____

3. On Wednesday, the boys brought more toys than the girls.

   How many more did they bring? _____ toys

4. On Thursday, the girls brought more toys than the boys.

   How many more did they bring? _____ toys

Read the pictograph. Answer the questions.

Buckets of Sand Filled

key
= 2 buckets

5. How many buckets did Nina fill? _____ buckets

6. How many buckets did Tom fill? _____ buckets

7. How many more buckets did Tom fill than Nina? _____ buckets

Review

Solve.

8.
$$\begin{array}{r} 95 \\ -\ 21 \\ \hline \end{array}$$

10.
$$\begin{array}{r} 62 \\ +\ 17 \\ \hline \end{array}$$

12.
$$\begin{array}{r} 34 \\ +\ 15 \\ \hline \end{array}$$

14.
$$\begin{array}{r} 60 \\ -\ 40 \\ \hline \end{array}$$

9.
$$\begin{array}{r} 88 \\ -\ 24 \\ \hline \end{array}$$

11.
$$\begin{array}{r} 33 \\ +\ 26 \\ \hline \end{array}$$

13.
$$\begin{array}{r} 75 \\ -\ 24 \\ \hline \end{array}$$

15.
$$\begin{array}{r} 99 \\ -\ 77 \\ \hline \end{array}$$

Dr. Vega studies sea animals. She counts the starfish in the tide pools. She made this graph to show how many starfish were in the tide pools in January, February, and March.

Starfish in Tide Pools

Fill in the correct circle.

1. How many starfish were in the tide pools in March?

   ○ 5   ○ 8   ○ 15   ○ 4

2. In which month did Dr. Vega see the fewest starfish?

   ○ January   ○ February   ○ March

3. Dr. Vega made a bar graph from the pictograph. Color the bar graph to match the pictograph.

Starfish in Tide Pools

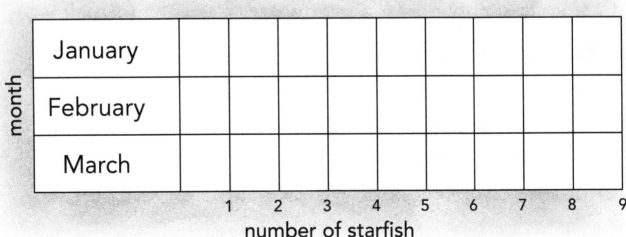

Read the map. Answer the questions.

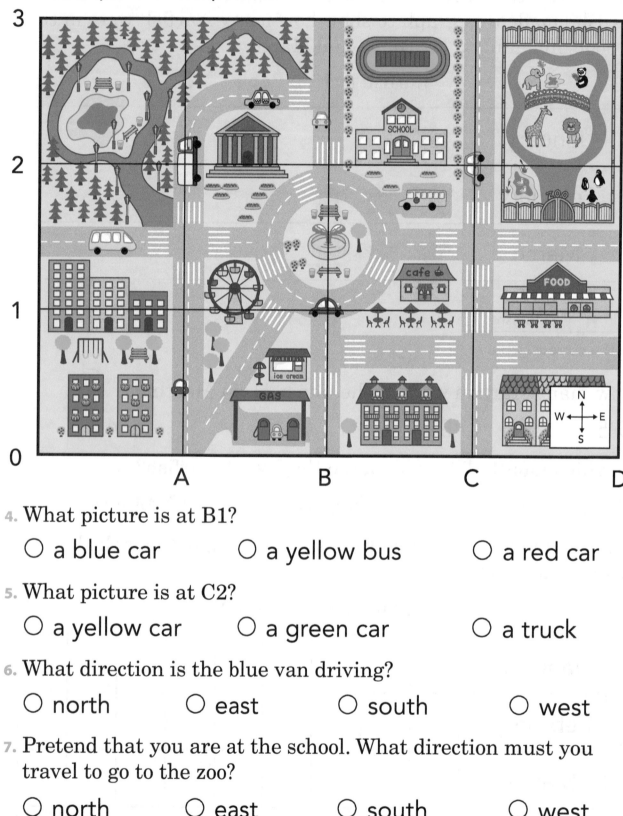

4. What picture is at B1?

   ○ a blue car   ○ a yellow bus   ○ a red car

5. What picture is at C2?

   ○ a yellow car   ○ a green car   ○ a truck

6. What direction is the blue van driving?

   ○ north   ○ east   ○ south   ○ west

7. Pretend that you are at the school. What direction must you
   travel to go to the zoo?

   ○ north   ○ east   ○ south   ○ west

Chapter 11
Problem Solving

The Lord does whatever pleases Him, in the heavens and on the earth, in the seas and all their depths.
Psalm 135:6

Key Ideas:

Measurement: comparison

Time: elapsed time

Money: estimation, comparison

Probability and Statistics: collecting and organizing data

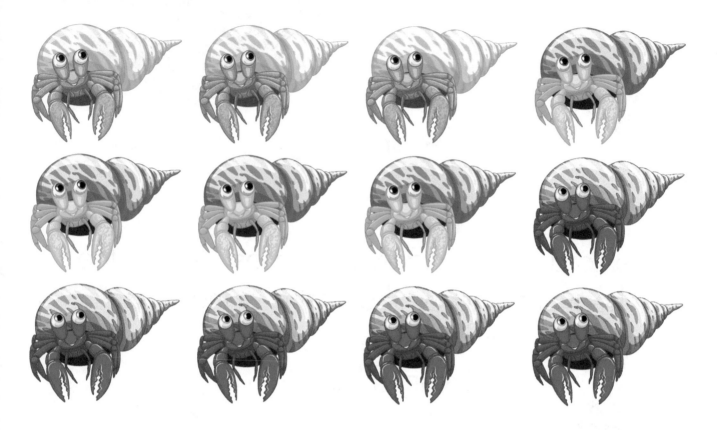

1. How many orange hermit crabs are there? _____

2. What is the total number of green hermit crabs and red hermit

   crabs? _____

3. How many more red hermit crabs are there than orange ones?

   _____

4. How many hermit crabs are there in all? _____

Draw a hermit crab of your own.

Read each word problem. Underline any clue words you see. Write the problem. Solve.

1. Kent went diving with his mom and dad. He saw 3 kinds of coral on Monday. On Tuesday, he saw 4 more kinds of coral. How many kinds of coral did he see in all?

tens	ones

_____ kinds of coral

2. There were 5 clown fish hiding in a reef. Then, 6 lion fish came along and hid. How many fish are hiding now?

tens	ones

_____ fish

3. Nara had 4 pieces of coral in her fish tank. Then, Nara's mom put 6 pieces of coral into the tank. How many pieces of coral are there altogether?

tens	ones

_____ pieces of coral

Read each word problem. Underline any clue words you see. Write the problem. Solve.

4. One coral reef is 8 miles long. Another reef is 4 miles long. What is the sum of the lengths of the two reefs?

	tens	ones

_____ miles

5. A ticket for the coral reef tour cost $24 for adults. For children, the price is $13. Lan and her mom each bought a ticket. What was the total price?

$

$

$

	tens	ones

_____ dollars

6. A diver measured coral. One piece was 7 feet wide. Another was 5 feet wide. What is the total width of both pieces of coral?

	tens	ones

_____ feet

7. Grandpa took 6 pictures of red coral, 3 of white coral, and 2 of brown coral. How many pictures did he take in all?

_____ pictures

	◯		◯		=	

Name _____

Read each word problem. Write the number sentence. Use the number line to solve.

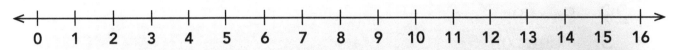

1. A sea snail, 2 clown fish, and 2 sea horses live on a coral reef. What is the total number of those sea animals?

   _____ sea animals

2. A group of 6 clown fish joined the 2 other clown fish. Now how many clown fish are there?

   _____ clown fish

Think about the number of hops needed to solve the problem. The first one is done for you.

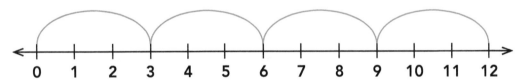

3. A sea horse can swim 3 feet in 1 minute. How far will the sea horse swim in 4 minutes?

   _____ feet

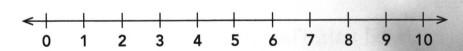

4. Some coral grows about 2 centimeters in a year. How much would it grow in 4 years?

   _____ centimeters

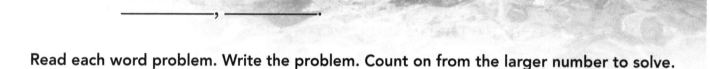

Count on to solve.

5.
$$29 \\ + \ 3 \over 32$$
Say 29.
Count on
30, 31, 32.

6.
$$81 \\ + \ 2$$
Say 81.
Count on

_____ , _____ .

Read each word problem. Write the problem. Count on from the larger number to solve.

7. A diver sees 39 green fish. She sees 4 red fish. How many fish does she see in all?

_____ fish
$$39 \\ + \ 4$$
Say 39.
Count on

_____ , _____ , _____ , _____ .

8. A school of 44 blue fish and a school of 6 pink fish swim over the reef. How many fish swim over the reef?

_____ fish

9. A submarine passes 47 striped fish. Then it passes 5 starfish. How many sea animals does it pass in all?

_____ sea animals

Name _____

Read each word problem. Underline any clue words. Write the problem. Solve.

1. Deon has a fish pond. He has 6 fish, but he would like to have 11 fish. How many more fish does he want?

   _____ fish

tens	ones

2. There were 8 fish in a stream. Then, 3 fish swam away. How many are left?

   _____ fish

tens	ones

  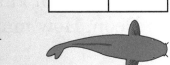

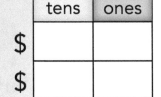

3. A goldfish costs $2, and a koi fish costs $10. What is the difference in cost?

   _____ dollars

tens	ones
$	
$	
$	

4. Wes had 11 cups of fish food. He fed his fish 2 cups. How many cups of fish food are left?

   _____ cups

tens	ones

Count back to solve.

5.
60 cars   Say 60.
− 3 cars   Count back
                  59, 58, 57.

7.
91
− 3

9.
70
− 2

6.
72 cars   Say 72.
− 2 cars   Count back

8.
42
− 3

10.
30
− 1

_____ , _____.

Count back to solve. Write the problem and the difference.

11. Costa's Koi Farm had 51 koi fish for sale. Mr. Costa sold 2 fish to Deon. How many fish are left?

_____ fish
51 fish   Say 51.
− 2 fish   Count back
49 fish   50, 49.

12. Mr. Costa buys 30-pound bags of koi food. Yesterday he fed his fish 3 pounds of food. How much food is left?

_____ pounds of food

tens	ones

Name _____

Write the number sentence. Count on to find the missing addend.

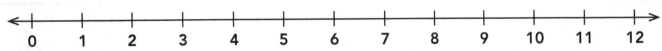

1. Pablo went to Sea Park to see the big fish tank. At 9 o'clock that morning, there were 8 sharks in the tank. At noon, Pablo counted 12 sharks. How many sharks were put into the tank between 9 o'clock and noon?

_____ sharks

[ ] + [ ] = [ ]

Write the number sentence. Use subtraction to find the missing addend.

2. The Sea Park staff began the day with 12 pails of fish. They fed the sea lions 5 pails in the morning. By evening, all 12 pails were empty. How many pails did the staff use that afternoon?

_____ pails

[ ] + [ ] = [ ]

3. A ticket to Sea Park costs $11. Jane paid $6 of her own money. Her mom paid the rest. How much did Jane's mom pay?

_____ dollars

$[ ] + $[ ] = $[ ]

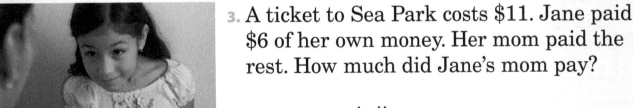

Subtract to find the missing addend.

4. A Sea Park T-shirt costs $25, but Ali only had $10. His brother gave him the rest of the money needed to buy the shirt. How much did Ali's brother give him?

$ ___10___ + $ [＿＿＿] = $ ___25___

	tens	ones
⊖	2	5
	1	0

Count on to find the missing addend.

5. Lexi wanted to buy a stuffed toy at Sea Park. The toy was $22 plus tax. Lexi paid $25. How much was the tax?

$ ___22___ + $ [＿＿＿] = $ ___25___

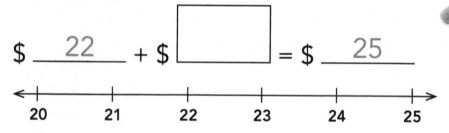

```
←—+———+———+———+———+———+—→
  20      21      22      23      24      25
```

Review

Add or subtract.

6.
```
   56
 − 21
```
[＿＿＿]

8.
```
   78
 − 36
```
[＿＿＿]

10.
```
   54
 + 12
```
[＿＿＿]

12.
```
   55
 − 23
```
[＿＿＿]

7.
```
   68
 + 11
```
[＿＿＿]

9.
```
   43
 + 24
```
[＿＿＿]

11.
```
   86
 − 26
```
[＿＿＿]

13.
```
   92
 − 71
```
[＿＿＿]

Name _____

Fill in the fact family. Read the problem. Solve it.

1. $3 + 5 = 8$ $8 - 3 = 5$

____ + ____ = 8   ____ − ____ = 3

Sasha found 5 pearls in the treasure chest. Then she found 3 rings. How many treasures did Sasha find altogether?

____ treasures

2. $6 + 4 = 10$ $10 - 6 = 4$

_____ + _____ = _____   _____ − _____ = _____

Anders had 10 coins. He gave 4 of them to his brother. How many coins does Anders have now?

____ coins

3. $10 + 6 = 16$ $16 - 10 = 6$

_____ + _____ = 16   _____ − _____ = 10

Lucy put 10 gold bars into the class treasure chest. Her teacher wants the chest to have 16 bars. How many more gold bars does Lucy need to put in?

____ gold bars

Complete the triangle flash cards for 12.

4.

Triangle	Top	Bottom left	Bottom right
	12	8	____
	12	3	____
	12	7	____
	12	6	____

Read and solve each problem.

5. Shannon wants to have 12 bushes in her garden. So far, she has planted 6. How many more bushes does she need to plant?

_____ flowers

6. Jimmy filled a box with 12 toy cars for his party guests. Eight friends came to the party and each took home a toy car. How many cars are left in the box?

_____ cars

7. Carly's pearl necklace broke. Three pearls were left on the string. Nine pearls fell to the floor. How many pearls were there in all?

_____ pearls

8. In Sal's desk, there are 7 pencils, 5 crayons, and 3 erasers. How many items are in his desk?

_____ items

Name _____

Read the information about Noah's ark. Write the problems. Solve.

1. God told Noah that the ark was to be 50 cubits wide and 30 cubits high. What is the difference between its width and height?

   _____ cubits

   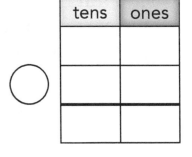

tens	ones

2. God told Noah to take 2 of every kind of animal. What is the sum of 2 rabbits, 2 frogs, and 2 cats?

   _____ animals   [ ] + [ ] + [ ] = [ ]

3. Noah, his wife, his 3 sons, their 3 wives, and all the animals went onto the ark. How many people lived on the ark in all?

   _____ people   [   ]

4. Rain fell on the earth for 40 days. About how much longer than one month did rain fall? Use a 30-day month.

   _____ days

   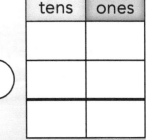

tens	ones

Fill in the circle for the combination that you would use to solve each word problem.

5. Jon Paul had 5 red cars and 7 blue cars in his toy box. How many cars did he have in all?

_____ cars

○ 5 + 7
○ 7 − 5
○ 12 − 5

6. Andrea lost her 12 new crayons. She found 6 of them. How many more does she need to find?

_____ crayons

○ 12 + 6
○ 12 − 6
○ 6 + 6

7. What is the difference between 11 and 7?

_____

○ 11 + 7
○ 11 − 7
○ 11 + 4

8. Titus sold 8 boxes of cookies to raise money for missions. If he sells 3 more boxes, how many will he have sold altogether?

_____ boxes

○ 8 − 3
○ 11 − 8
○ 8 + 3

9. Nate has an aquarium with 6 red fish, 4 blue fish, and 2 orange fish. How many fish are in Nate's aquarium?

_____ fish

○ 6 + 42
○ 6 + 4 + 2
○ 64 + 2

10. When 4 is added to a number, the total is 9. What is the number?

_____

○ 9 + 4
○ ▢ + 4 = 9
○ 4 + 9

Read the problem. Mark off any information you do not need. Solve the problem.

1. Jonah went fishing. He wanted to catch 10 fish for dinner. He caught 3. He brought 12 worms. How many more fish does Jonah need to catch?

_____ fish

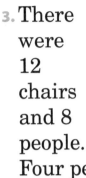

3. There were 12 chairs and 8 people. Four people brought lunches. How many more chairs than people were there?

_____ chairs

2. The pool was 89°F in the morning and 99°F in the afternoon. The swim class started at 3:30. How much did the water temperature change?

_____ °F

4. There were 17 umbrellas. A strong wind blew 6 down. Seven people sat in the chairs. How many umbrellas were still standing?

_____ umbrellas

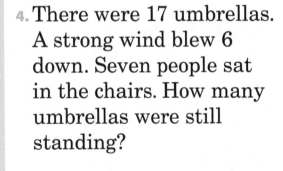

Read the problem. Mark off any information you do not need. Solve the problem.

5. The vendor had 55 ice cream bars to sell. He sold 31. How many bars were left?

_____ bars

6. Twelve seagulls looked for clams. Nine seagulls found clams. Six sandpipers ate flies. How many seagulls did not find clams?

_____ seagulls

7. There were 10 pink jellyfish. The blue boat had 6 sails. There were 9 clear jellyfish. How many jellyfish were there in all?

_____ jellyfish

8. An airplane had a 20-foot banner. Another plane had a 32-foot banner. How much longer is the second banner?

_____ feet

Read the problem. Solve it.

1. Peter penguin is 45 inches tall.
Patty penguin is 24 inches tall.
What is the difference?

   _____ inches

Peter 45 inches tall

2. Paul penguin is 20 inches tall.
Which penguin is taller, Patty or
Paul?

   _____

   How much taller?

   _____ inches

Patty 24 inches tall

3. If Patty penguin stood on the head
of Paul penguin, would they be
taller than Peter penguin?

   _____

Paul 20 inches tall

4. Penny penguin is 18 inches tall.
How many more inches would
Penny need to grow to be as tall as
Paul?

   _____ inches

Penny 18 inches tall

Read the problem. Solve it.

5. It was 59°F in the afternoon.
   It changed to 39°F at night.
   How much did the temperature change?

   _____ °F

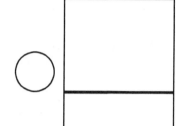

6. Mrs. Brown has one quart of milk.
   She wants to give her four boys one cup each.
   Does she have enough milk?

   _____

quart

7. There were 16 bowls of soup. Eight people each had one bowl of soup. How many bowls of soup are left?

   _____ bowls

8. Pedro ran 15 yards. Kylie ran 15 meters. Who ran farther?

   _____

   yard

   meter

Name _____

Read the problem. Solve it.

1. One foot of ribbon costs 30¢.
   What is the cost for 3 feet?

   _____ cents

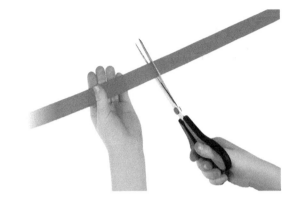

2. Brett gave 20¢ at church.
   His sister gave 15¢.
   How much did they give altogether?

   _____ cents

3. Carla bought a coloring book. It cost $1.30.
   She gave the clerk $1.50.
   How much change did she get?

   _____ cents

4. A gallon of milk sold for $3.39.
   A dozen eggs sold for $2.09.
   What was the difference?

   $ _____ . _____

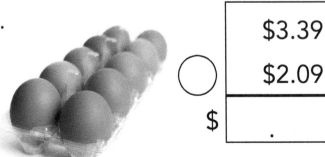

$3.39

$2.09

$ _____ .

Read the problem. Solve it.

5. You have 1 dime, 1 nickel, and 4 pennies. Pencils cost 5¢ each. How many could you buy?

_____ pencils

6. Dylan had $1.45. He lost three coins. Now he only has $1.25. How much money did he lose?

_____ cents

7. Kai had eight quarters. He kept two quarters and shared the rest with three friends. Now they each have two coins. How much does each boy have now?

_____ cents

Review

Write the numbers in expanded form.

8. 354 _____ + _____ + ____

9. 623 _____ + _____ + ____

Add.

10.
$$\begin{array}{r} 354 \\ +623 \\ \hline \end{array}$$

Name _____

Time **11.10**

1. Circle the month that comes first in the calendar. Underline the month that comes last. Cross out the 10th month of the year. Draw a square around the 6th month.

December   January   June   October   March

2. Write the days of the week in order.

_____

_____

_____

_____

_____

_____

_____

Read and answer.

3. The year began on a Tuesday. Jared was born three days later. On what day of the week was Jared born?

_____ What was his birth date?

_____

4. Jared was born at 8:45. Draw the time on the clock.

5. Lily, Jared's sister, got to see him three hours later.

What time was it then? _____

Read the problem. Solve it.

6. It is 3:30. Viv has to practice piano for 15 minutes. What time will it be when she is finished?

_____ : _____

7. The clock showed:

Maddox ran around the track two times. When he finished, the clock showed:

How much time did Maddox spend running?

_____ minutes

8. Dana practiced her cartwheels for 15 minutes. When she finished, it was 8:45. What time did she start?

_____ : _____

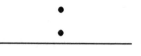

9. Joseph practices violin for 30 minutes each night. He always starts at 6:45. What time is it when he is done?

_____ : _____

Name _____

Read and solve the word problems.

1. Malia has 16 dolls. Amber has 12. How many dolls do they have altogether?

   _____ dolls

3. Christian has 19 teeth. His baby brother has 3. How many more teeth does Christian have than his brother?

   _____ teeth

2. Jayla read two picture books. One has 16 pages. The other one has 20. How many pages did Jayla read?

   _____ pages

4. Victor is the goalkeeper for his team. He stopped 3 balls in the first half of the game and 6 in the second half. How many balls did he stop?

   _____ balls

Read and solve the word problems.

5. Dixon measured his foot. It is 19 centimeters long. The widest part of his foot is 8 centimeters wide. How much longer is his foot than it is wide?

_____ centimeters

6. Alberto liked to count. He counted 35 steps from his bedroom to the kitchen. He counted 42 steps from the kitchen to the front door. How many steps did he take altogether?

_____ steps

Add or subtract.

7. The temperature was 10°C. It warmed up to 25°C. How much did it change?

8. The temperature was 68°F. It cooled off to 32°F. How much did it change?

°C
°C
°C

°F
°F
°F

Draw a picture to help you solve the problem.

1. Far from the beach, 10 dolphins swam in a pod. Then, 3 went to swim around the boat. How many dolphins were left?

_____ dolphins

2. At snack time 4 children shared 10 cookies. How many cookies did each child get?

_____ cookies

3. Write a sentence explaining your last answer.

_____

_____

Draw a picture to help you solve the problem.

4. The 3 lighthouses each had 5 lights. How many lights were there in all?

_____ lights

5. If it took 10 minutes to light 2 lanterns, how long would it take to light 8 lanterns?

_____ minutes

6. There were 12 seashells on the beach. If 4 friends shared them equally, how many shells would each friend have?

_____ shells

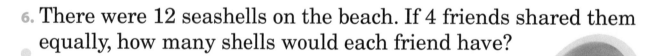

Name _____

Probability is the chance that something might happen.

Read each word problem. Use the information in the problem to make your best guess. Circle your choice.

1. Adam has a bag with 10 white checkers and 5 black checkers. He asks his dad to take a checker without looking. What color checker is his dad most likely to pick?

white   black

2. Cruz has a package of gummy bears. He knows the package has 7 red bears, 3 yellow bears, 3 green bears, and 1 orange bear. If Cruz takes a gummy bear out of the package without looking, what color is he most likely to choose?

red   yellow   orange   green

3. Luna has a bag of marbles. She has 12 blue ones, 3 yellow ones, and 2 green ones. If Luna pulls one marble from the bag, what is the most likely color?

yellow   green   blue

Read the word problem. Circle your choice.

4. Mrs. Cho is drying socks. She put 4 pink socks, 2 black socks, and 10 gray socks in the dryer. If she pulls a sock from the dryer without looking, which color is she most likely to pull?

pink   black   gray

If Mrs. Cho is making pairs of socks from the socks listed above, what color sock would likely be the first pair she can make?

Write the color on the line. _____

Make tally marks in the table. Answer the questions.

5. Flip a penny 10 times. Tally each time.

heads	
tails	

How many times did it land heads up? _____ times

How many times did it land tails up? _____ time

What will the penny land on next? _____

Flip the penny once more. Was your guess correct?

yes   no

Name _____

To estimate is to make a close guess.

Fill in the circle in front of the best estimate. Then, find the exact answer.

1. Kendra had a bag of 49 colored candies. She ate 38 candies. About how many are left?

   ○ 5 candies
   ○ 40 candies
   ○ 10 candies

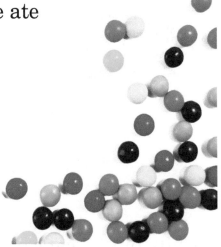

2. Grandpa Jones grows oranges. He has 2 trees. Last year, each tree grew 24 oranges. About how many oranges will grow on the trees altogether this year?

   ○ 50 oranges
   ○ 100 oranges
   ○ 25 oranges

3. Mario's small fishbowl can hold 9 fish. Mario wants a bowl twice as big. About how many fish can the larger bowl hold?

   ○ 10 fish
   ○ 20 fish
   ○ 40 fish

Fill in the circle in front of the best estimate. Then, find the exact answer.

4. Ty's family travels 10 miles to Happy City. Then, they drive 19 miles farther. About how far is Ty from home?

○ 60 miles
○ 30 miles
○ 10 miles

5. Cally put 22 cans of food into a box for the shelter. She wants to fill another box. The boxes are the same size. About how many cans of food can she pack into the 2 boxes altogether?

○ 140 cans
○ 20 cans
○ 40 cans

Review

Write the missing addends.

6. 7 + ____ = 11

7. 5 + ____ = 11

8. 3 + ____ = 10

9. ____ + 4 = 12

10. ____ + 3 = 12

11. 6 + ____ = 10

12. ____ + 5 = 12

13. 7 + ____ = 9

14. 8 + ____ = 11

15. 9 + ____ = 10

16. 6 + ____ = 12

17. 9 + ____ = 11

Read the word problem. Look for clue words. Draw a picture or write a problem to solve.

1. Janie watched a sailboat race. Ten boats started the race. Janie saw 8 boats cross the finish line. How many boats are left?

   _____ boats

2. Mr. Ravel and his son are in the sailboat race. They plan to sail 25 miles. They have gone 10 miles. How many more miles do they have to go?

   _____ miles

3. The red sail is 26 feet high. The white sail is 24 feet high. What is the difference?

   _____ feet

4. The sailboat race started at the time shown on the clock. It lasted 2 hours. What time did the race end?

   _____

Write the problem. Solve.

5. The longest boat in the race was 40 feet. The shortest boat was 29 feet. What is the total length of the two boats?

_____ feet

6. Mrs. López bought a ticket to the boat race. She paid $8 for the ticket plus tax. The total came to $10. How much was the tax?

_____ dollars   _____ + _____ = _____

7. Mari saw 15 red boats, 26 white boats, and 2 blue boats in the race. Which color boat is most likely to win? Use probability.

○ a red boat   ○ a white boat   ○ a blue boat

Read the word problem. Color the boats in order. Solve.

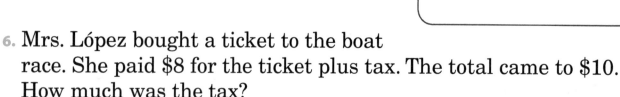

8. A red boat is 7 meters ahead of a blue boat. The blue boat is 5 meters ahead of a white boat. How far is the white boat from the red boat?

_____ meters

Which fact family would you use to solve the word problem?

○ 7 + 5 = 12   ○ 5 + 2 = 7   ○ 7 + 2 = 9
  5 + 7 = 12   2 + 5 = 7   2 + 7 = 9
  12 − 5 = 7   7 − 5 = 2   9 − 2 = 7
  12 − 7 = 5   7 − 2 = 5   9 − 7 = 2

Name _____

Find the area of each shape in square centimeters.

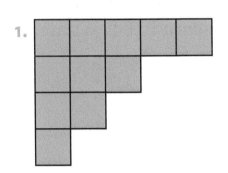

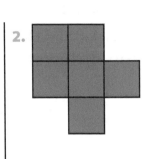

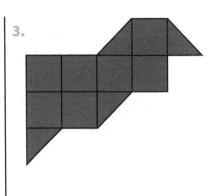

1. _____ square cm

2. _____ square cm

3. _____ square cm

Match the name to the picture.

4. Bar graph ●

5. Venn diagram ●

6. Pictograph ●

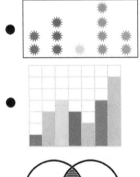

Read the graph. Solve.

7. What is the object at C3? _____

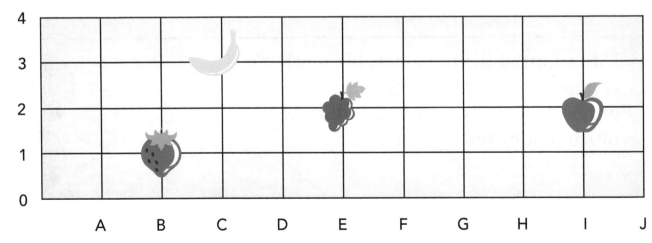

Read the word problem. Solve it.

8. Riley scored 263 points in the video game. Last time, she scored 151. What is the difference?

_____ points

9. Malala has 12 beads on her bracelet. Aria has 14 on hers. How many beads are there altogether?

_____ beads

10. The train arrived at 7:15. The next train leaves at 7:45. How much time is there between the two trains?

_____ minutes

11. Vito counted the money in his mother's change purse. She had 2 quarters, 3 dimes, 3 pennies, and 1 nickel. How much money did she have?

_____ ¢

Chapter 12
Cumulative Review

"Come, follow Me," Jesus said, "and I will send you out to fish for people."
Matthew 4:19

Key Ideas:

Review and reinforcement of skills and concepts taught in Grade 1

Match.

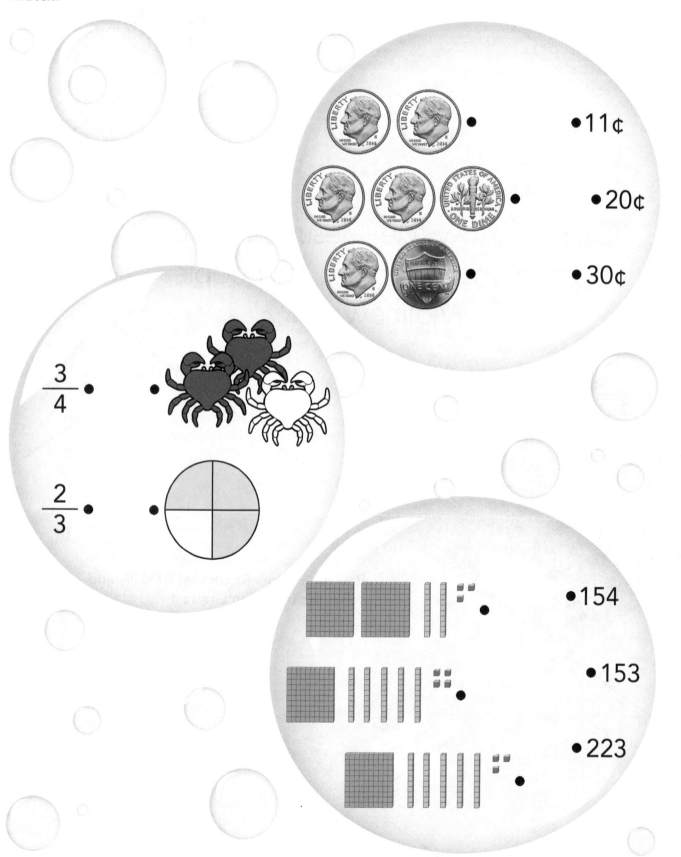

Name _____

Color an AB pattern on the seashells. Color an ABC pattern on the fish.

1.

2.

Write the numbers.

3. Odd numbers to 19 _____, _____, _____, _____, _____,

_____, _____, _____, _____

4. Even numbers to 20 _____, _____, _____, _____, _____,

_____, _____, _____, _____

5. The letter A stands for a sailboat, B stands for a fish, and C stands for a starfish. Begin at the first sailboat in the top row. Trace an AABC pattern on the grid.

Match each word to its meaning.

6. pattern • • a series that repeats over and over

7. number • • a symbol that stands for a number

8. numeral • • a word that tells how many

Fill in the circle that shows a rotation (spin) of the first shape.

1.

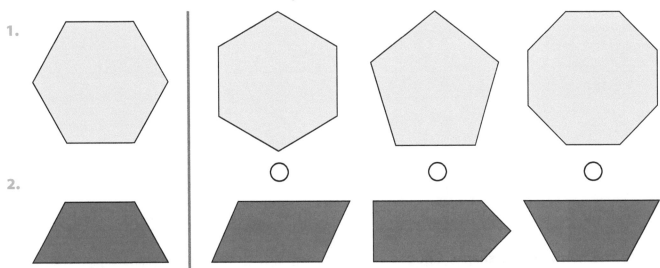

2.

Fill in the circle that shows a translation (slide) of the first shape.

3.

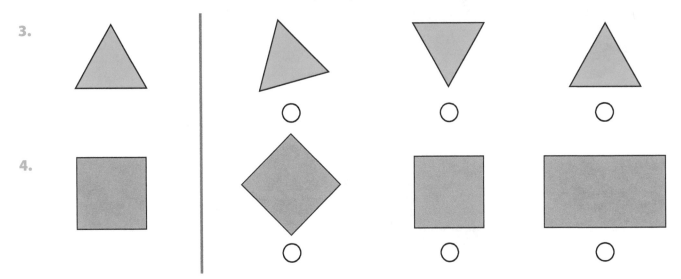

4.

Fill in the circle that shows a reflection (flip) of the first shape.

5.

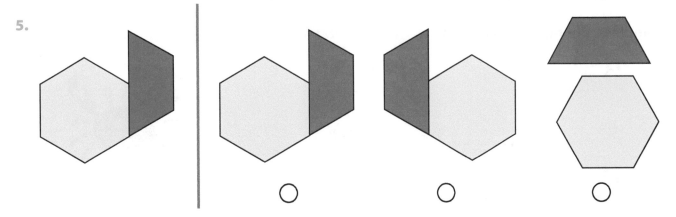

Draw the other half of each figure to show symmetry.

6.
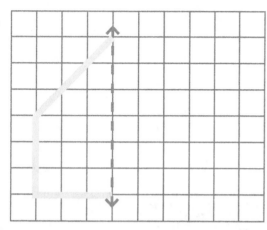

7.
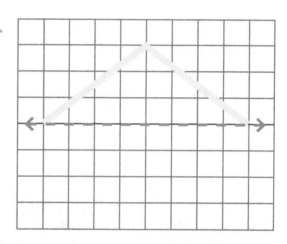

Write the name of the shape. Choose rhombus, square, circle, rectangle, triangle, **or** oval.

8.

10.

12.

_____   _____   _____

9.

11.

13.

_____   _____   _____

Complete the number patterns.

14. __0__, __5__, __10__, _____, _____, _____

15. __30__, _____, __50__, _____, __70__

16. __13__, __15__, _____, __19__

Name _____

Add or subtract.

1.   8
   + 4

3.   2
   + 8

5.   9
   − 8

7.   10
   − 4

9.   3
   + 3

2.   4
   + 6

4.   2
   + 9

6.   5
   − 1

8.   7
   − 4

10.   8
    − 5

Read each word problem. Draw a picture or write a number sentence to solve it.

11. Melanie and Mitt Carter are twins. They live with Mom, Dad, and Grandma. When the twins set the table, how many plates do they need?

_____ plates

12. Mrs. Carter made big meatballs. She made 3 meatballs each for herself, for Dad, and for Grandma. She made 1 meatball for each child. How many meatballs did she make?

_____ meatballs

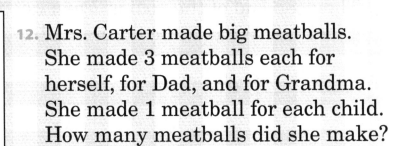

Write the missing numerals. Then, write the fact family for each set of facts.

13.

___ + ___ = ___

___ + ___ = ___

___ − ___ = ___

___ − ___ = ___

14.

___ + ___ = ___

___ + ___ = ___

___ − ___ = ___

___ − ___ = ___

15.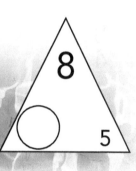

___ + ___ = ___

___ + ___ = ___

___ − ___ = ___

___ − ___ = ___

Solve the word problems.

16. Three swimmers were in the pool. They each did 4 laps. How many laps did they swim altogether?

___ + ___ + ___ = _____ laps

17. The deep end of the pool is 7 feet deep. The tallest swimmer is 4 feet tall. What is the difference?

_____ feet

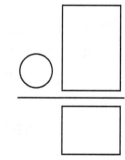

Cut out the coins. Make each amount. Glue the coins in place.

1.  31¢

2. 8¢

3. 26¢

4.  15¢

5. 30¢

6.  20¢

Write the amount.

7. = _____ ¢

8. = _____ ¢

9. = _____ ¢

10. = _____ ¢

Tyler is setting the clock for his friend.
He wants his clock to show 6:30.

1. Show 6:30 on this clock.

6:30

Write the time. Draw hands to show 1 hour later than the first time shown. Write the new time.

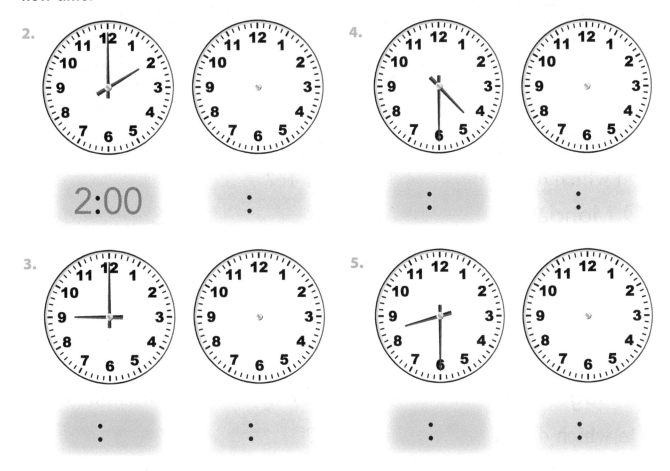

2.   2:00

3.

4.

5.

Write the time. Then, draw the hands on the second clock to show 1 hour earlier than the time shown. Write the new time.

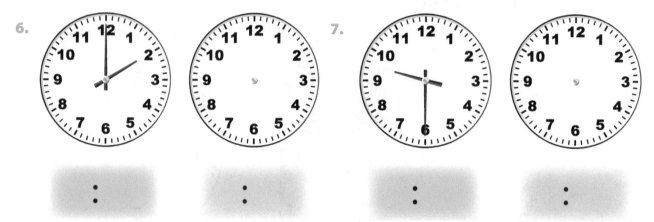

6.

7.

Read the calendars. Fill in the circles to answer the questions.

JULY						
S	M	T	W	TH	F	S
				1	2	3
4	5	6	7	8	9	10
11	12	13	14	15	16	17
18	19	20	21	22	23	24
25	26	27	28	29	30	31

AUGUST						
S	M	T	W	TH	F	S
1	2	3	4	5	6	7
8	9	10	11	12	13	14
15	16	17	18	19	20	21
22	23	24	25	26	27	28
29	30	31				

8. On which day of the week is August 15?

○ Monday   ○ Tuesday   ○ Sunday

9. How many Tuesdays are in July?

○ 5   ○ 4   ○ 3

10. Josh's birthday is on the last Saturday in August. What is the date of his birthday?

○ August 28   ○ August 29   ○ August 31

11. On which day of the week is July 4?

○ Sunday   ○ Wednesday   ○ Monday

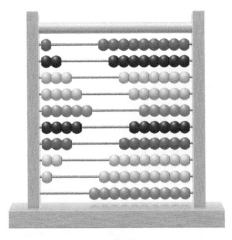

100
one set of one hundred

10
one set of 10

1
one

Write the amount.

1.

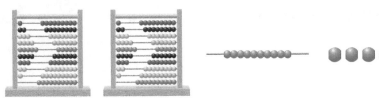

= _____

2.

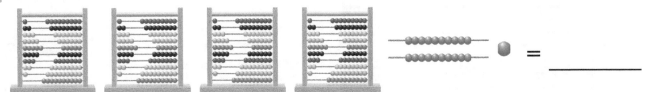

= _____

3.

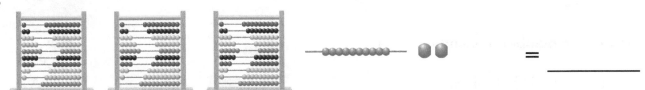

= _____

4.

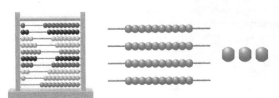

= _____

Match the picture to the correct amount.

5.  •   • 340

6.   •   • 304

7.   •   • 646

8.   •   • 138

Write each number in standard form.

9. $100 + 10 + 1 =$ _____

10. $400 + 70 + 6 =$ _____

11. $90 + 2 =$ _____

12. $80 + 5 =$ _____

Name _____

The Statue of Liberty stands in New York Harbor. The statue is 151 feet tall!

Answer the questions.

1. Each of the Statue of Liberty's eyes is 30 inches. Find 30 inches on a yardstick. Put a counter on 30 inches. Count on to the end of the yardstick. How many inches did you count?

   _____ inches

2. The statue's waist is 35 feet wide. The feet are 25 feet long. What is the difference between the two measurements? Write the problem. Solve.

   _____ feet

Choose a partner to help you measure. Use a tape measure.

3. The Statue of Liberty's nose is 54 inches long. How long is your nose?

   _____ inches

4. Liberty's arm is 42 feet long. How long is your arm?

   _____ inches

5. One of Liberty's fingers is 8 feet long. How long is one of your fingers?

   _____ inches

Measure the picture of the statue with a ruler. Fill in the blanks.

6. In the picture, the Statue of Liberty's arm and

   torch together are _____ centimeters.

7. The picture is _____ centimeters from the
   statue's crown to her feet.

Measure the lines.

8.

├─────────────────────┤   _____ inches

9.

├─────────────┤   _____ centimeters

10.

├──────┤   _____ inches

11.

├────────────────────────┤   _____ centimeters

12.

├───────────┤   _____ inches

Name _____

Capacity is the amount a container can hold. Different containers have different capacities.

Fill in the circle under the container that has greater capacity.

1. ○   ○   2. ○   ○   3. ○   ○

Fill in the circle under the container that has less capacity.

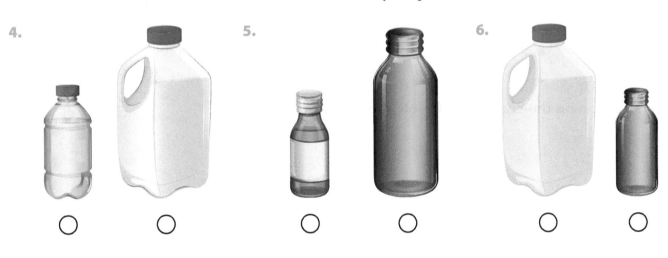

4. ○   ○   5. ○   ○   6. ○   ○

7. **Color 1 cup.**

8. **Color $\frac{2}{3}$ cup.**

9. **Color $\frac{1}{2}$ cup.**

Fill in the correct circle.

10. Which scale shows that the bananas are heavier?

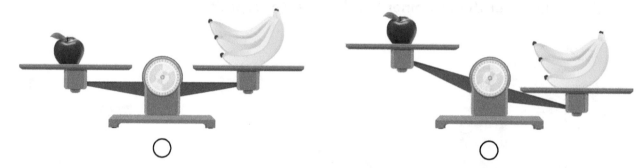

○   ○

11. Which scale shows that the lemon is lighter?

○   ○

Draw items on the scales that weigh about the same.

12.   **13.**

Review

Add or subtract.

14.	15.	16.	17.	18.	19.
7 + 4	48 − 6	27 + 32	45 − 15	6 + 4	5 + 6

Name _____

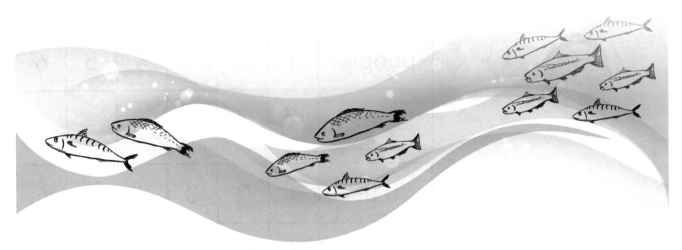

1. **Look at the fish swimming down the river. The pattern is written for you. Fill in the number pattern.**

| 2 | 4 | 6 | | | Pattern: __count by twos__

Fill in the number pattern. Write the pattern.

2.

| 0 | 5 | 10 | | | Pattern: _____

3.

| 1 | 4 | 7 | | | Pattern: _____

4.

| 3 | 7 | 11 | | | Pattern: _____

Find the number pattern. Fill in the circle under the missing number.

5.

44   46   ___   50   42   52   48
                           ○   ○   ○

6.

29   31   ___   35   37   39   33   32
                           ○   ○   ○

Look for a pattern. Complete the table.

7.

people	1	2	3	4	5	6
eyes	2	4				

8.

feet	1	2	3	4	5	6
toes	5	10				

9.

triangles	1	2	3	4	5	6
sides	3	6				

10.

squares	1	2	3	4	5	6
sides	4	8				

Add or subtract.

11.
$$\begin{array}{r} 4 \\ -\ 3 \\ \hline \end{array}$$

13.
$$\begin{array}{r} 4 \\ +\ 2 \\ \hline \end{array}$$

15.
$$\begin{array}{r} 12 \\ -\ 8 \\ \hline \end{array}$$

17.
$$\begin{array}{r} 5 \\ +\ 6 \\ \hline \end{array}$$

19.
$$\begin{array}{r} 90 \\ +\ 8 \\ \hline \end{array}$$

12.
$$\begin{array}{r} 4 \\ +\ 8 \\ \hline \end{array}$$

14.
$$\begin{array}{r} 9 \\ -\ 6 \\ \hline \end{array}$$

16.
$$\begin{array}{r} 45 \\ +\ 12 \\ \hline \end{array}$$

18.
$$\begin{array}{r} 11 \\ +\ 7 \\ \hline \end{array}$$

20.
$$\begin{array}{r} 33 \\ -\ 11 \\ \hline \end{array}$$

Draw a line to divide each shape in half. Color $\frac{1}{2}$.

1.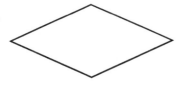

2.

3.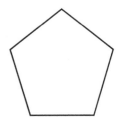

Color $\frac{1}{3}$ of each shape.

4.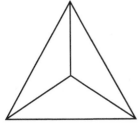

5.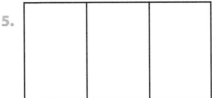

6.

Color $\frac{3}{4}$ of each shape.

7.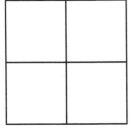

8.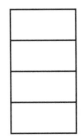

9.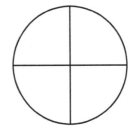

10.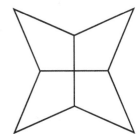

Look at the fish. Answer each question.

  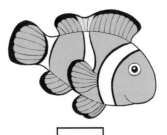 

11. What fraction of the fish is orange? $\frac{\square}{\square}$

12. What fraction is green? $\frac{\square}{\square}$

13. What fraction is blue? $\frac{\square}{\square}$

Solve. Use the pictures to help you.

14. Cindy saw 6 shells on the sand. She picked up $\frac{1}{2}$ of them. How many are left on the sand?

_____ shells

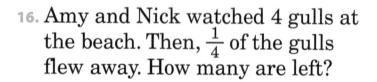

15. Pat and his friend Sandy rode their bikes to the beach. One tire went flat. What fraction of the tires was flat?

 of the tires

16. Amy and Nick watched 4 gulls at the beach. Then, $\frac{1}{4}$ of the gulls flew away. How many are left?

_____ gulls

17. Three dolphins swam close to shore. Then, 2 dolphins swam away. Write a fraction to tell how many swam away.

of the dolphins

Solve.

1. Jonathan wants to buy a plant for his mother. The plant costs 99 cents. He has 79 cents in one pocket and 2 dimes in another pocket. Does he have enough to buy the plant?

$$
\begin{array}{r}
7\ 9\ ¢ \\
+\ \ \ \ \ ¢ \\
\hline
¢
\end{array}
$$

Add or subtract.

2.
	5 tens	3 ones
−	2 tens	1 one
	tens	ones

3.
	4 tens	5 ones
+	4 tens	2 ones
	tens	ones

4.
$$
\begin{array}{r}
26¢ \\
+\ 42¢ \\
\hline
¢
\end{array}
$$

6.
$$
\begin{array}{r}
81¢ \\
-\ 10¢ \\
\hline
¢
\end{array}
$$

8.
$$
\begin{array}{r}
17¢ \\
+\ 22¢ \\
\hline
¢
\end{array}
$$

10.
$$
\begin{array}{r}
65¢ \\
-\ 14¢ \\
\hline
¢
\end{array}
$$

5.
$$
\begin{array}{r}
59¢ \\
-\ 33¢ \\
\hline
¢
\end{array}
$$

7.
$$
\begin{array}{r}
47¢ \\
-\ 11¢ \\
\hline
¢
\end{array}
$$

9.
$$
\begin{array}{r}
35¢ \\
-\ \ 3¢ \\
\hline
¢
\end{array}
$$

11.
$$
\begin{array}{r}
28¢ \\
+\ 31¢ \\
\hline
¢
\end{array}
$$

Read and solve the word problems.

12. Andy has 3 dimes and 5 pennies. He wants to buy a balloon that costs 25¢. Does he have enough money?

_____

13. Jamie and Kristy put their money together. They had 54¢ and 35¢. How much do they have altogether?

_____ ¢

14. Bryce read his favorite book 3 days in a row. Each day he read for 10 minutes. How much time did he read in all?

_____ minutes

Write the numbers.

15.   4 tens   6 ones

16.   6 tens   5 ones

17.   7 tens   2 ones

18.   2 tens   0 ones

Seashells Found

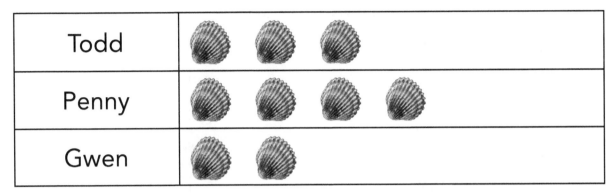

Todd	
Penny	
Gwen	

 = 2 seashells

Read the pictograph. Answer the questions.

1. How many seashells did Gwen find? _____ seashells

2. How many seashells did Todd find? _____ seashells

3. Who found the most shells? _____

4. What is the difference between the greatest number and the least

   number of shells found? _____ seashells

5. Color the bar graph to match the pictograph. Remember, each space on the bar graph stands for one seashell.

Seashells Found

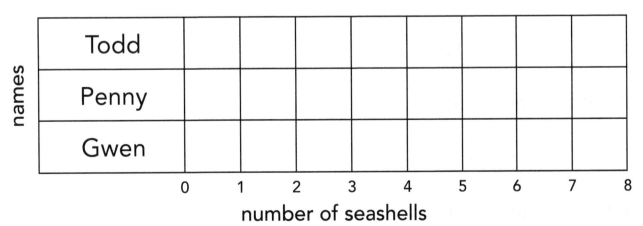

number of seashells

Read the coordinate graph.

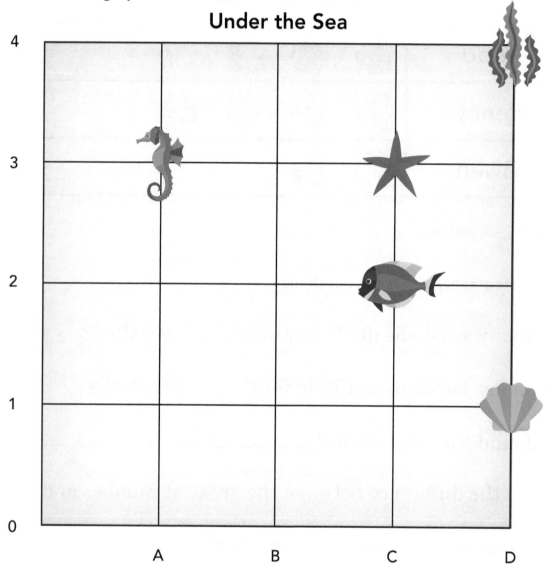

Under the Sea

Answer the questions.

6. What is at point A3? _____

7. What is at point D4? _____

8. What is at point C3? _____

9. What is at point C2? _____

10. What is at point D1? _____

Name _____

Solve the word problems. Draw a picture or write the problem.

1. Peter walked along the shore each evening for 32 days. He missed seeing the sunset 2 times. How many times did Peter see the sunset?

_____ times

2. Jed has 2 gray bricks, 6 black ones, and 3 blue ones. How many bricks are there in all?

_____ bricks

3. Lee Ann got to the bus stop at 7:15. The bus came at 7:30. How long did she wait for the bus?

_____ minutes

4. Oliver is 48 inches tall now that he is a first grader. When he was born, he was only 18 inches long. What is the difference between his length at birth and his height now?

_____ inches

Solve the word problems. Draw a picture or write the problem.

5. A balloon seller had 4 blue balloons, 3 red ones, and 5 yellow ones. How many balloons did he have in all?

_____ balloons

6. Saka looked under the sofa. She found 2 quarters, 2 dimes, 2 nickels, 4 pennies, 3 buttons, and 1 pencil. How much money did she find?

_____ cents

7. Alfred played soccer for 12 minutes. For 7 minutes, he played goalie. The rest of the time, Alfred played guard. How many minutes did Alfred play as a guard?

_____ minutes

8. How many different triangles are in this flag? Color each different triangle you find. Count all the triangles.

_____ triangles

Write the numerals. Circle the odd numerals.

1. _____

eighteen ---------------- _____

2. _____

twelve ---------------- _____

3. _____

thirteen ---------------- _____

4. _____

two ---------------- _____

5. _____

fifteen ---------------- _____

6. _____

nine ---------------- _____

7. Match the shapes.

•   •   •   •

•   •   •   •

oval   square   trapezoid   rhombus

Continue the counting pattern.

8. 2, 4, 6, 8, 10, _____, _____, _____, _____

9. 15, 20, 25, 30, _____, _____, _____, _____

Complete the fact family. Use only the numbers on the kites.

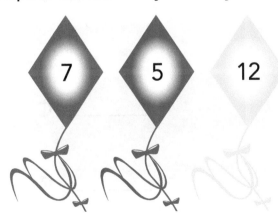

10. _____ + _____ = _____

11. _____ + _____ = _____

12. _____ − _____ = _____

13. _____ − _____ = _____

Choose the correct answer. Fill in the circle.

14.
$$9$$
$$+ \ 3$$

ⓐ 12

ⓑ 11

ⓒ 6

16.
$$7$$
$$+ \ 3$$

ⓐ 10

ⓑ 2

ⓒ 4

15.
$$11$$
$$- \ 7$$

ⓐ 6

ⓑ 5

ⓒ 4

17.
$$10$$
$$- \ 6$$

ⓐ 5

ⓑ 4

ⓒ 8

Add.

18. $3 + 4 + 4 =$ _____

20. $7 + 2 + 0 =$ _____

19. $2 + 1 + 3 =$ _____

21. $5 + 5 + 2 =$ _____

Show the time.

22.

3:00

23.

4:30

24.

6:15

Count the money.

25.

= _____ ¢

26.

= _____ ¢

Name _____

Write the number.

27. 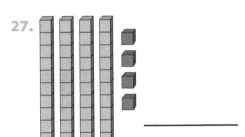 _____

28. 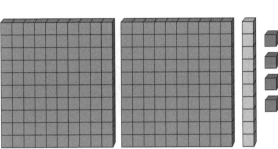 _____

Write in standard form.

29. 40 + 3 = _____   31. 600 + 20 + 5 = _____

30. 70 + 2 = _____   32. 500 + 80 + 4 = _____

33. **Write the numbers in order from least to greatest.**

78   87   23   6   12   32

____   ____   ____   ____   ____   ____

Circle the place value of the underlined digit.

34. 4<u>5</u>6   hundreds   tens   ones

35. 89<u>3</u>   hundreds   tens   ones

Measure each object.

36.

_____ centimeters

37.

_____ inches

Write the fraction for the colored part.

38. 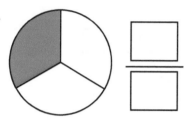 $\dfrac{}{}$

39. 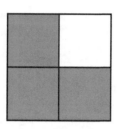 $\dfrac{}{}$

40.  $\dfrac{}{}$

Solve.

41.
$$\begin{array}{r} 33 \\ + \ 26 \\ \hline \end{array}$$

42.
$$\begin{array}{r} 98 \\ - \ 25 \\ \hline \end{array}$$

43.
$$\begin{array}{r} 42 \\ + \ 13 \\ \hline \end{array}$$

Write the missing addends.

44. $6 + \underline{} = 12$

45. $5 + \underline{} = 11$

Read the graph. Answer the questions.

The pictograph shows the number of Bible verses that a first-grade class learned.

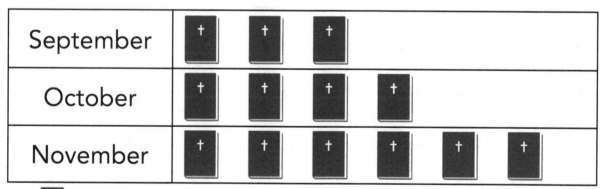

† = 2 verses

46. In which month did the first graders learn just 6 verses?

_____

47. How many more verses did the first graders learn in November than in September?

_____ verses

Time

1 hour = 60 minutes
1 day = 24 hours
1 week = 7 days
1 year = 12 months

United States Customary Units

Length
1 foot = 12 inches
1 yard = 3 feet

Weight
pound

Capacity
1 pint = 2 cups
1 quart = 2 pints
1 gallon = 4 quarts

Metric Units

Length
centimeter

Weight
kilogram

Capacity
liter

Money

1 penny = 1 cent (¢)
1 nickel = 5 cents
1 dime = 10 cents
1 quarter = 25 cents
1 dollar ($) = 100 cents

Symbols

< is less than
> is greater than
= is equal to

add
page 65

to combine two or more numbers

2   +   3   =   5

addend
page 65

a number that is added to another number

② + ③ = 5

area
page 299

the number of square units needed to cover a surface

centimeter
page 163

a unit of measurement in the metric system

circle
page 175

a perfectly round shape

cup
page 175

a customary unit used to measure liquids or solids

degree
page 181

a unit of measurement for temperature

difference
page 87

the answer to a subtraction problem

5   –   3   =   ②

digit page 133

any of the numerals 0–9

estimate page 341

to make a close guess

dime page 113

10 cents

even number page 26

a number that can be divided into sets of two with no leftovers

dollar page 119

100 cents

foot page 167

a customary unit of measurement that equals 12 inches

equal page 47

having the same number

  =

fourth page 229

one part of a whole that has been divided into four equal parts

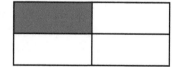

fraction
page 223

a part of a whole

half
page 225

one part of a whole that has been divided into two equal parts

gallon
page 175

an amount equal to four quarts

hexagon
page 33

a shape with six sides

graph
page 287

a chart that shows information

hour hand
page 101

the shorter hand used to tell the hour on a clock

greater than
page 212

a number or amount that is more than another number or amount

inch
page 161

a unit of measurement in the customary system

kilogram   page 180

a metric unit used to measure weight

minus   page 69

to subtract

5   $-$ 3   =   2

less than   page 212

a number or amount that is smaller than another number or amount

3   <   10

minute hand   page 101

the longer hand used to tell the minutes on a clock

liter   page 177

a metric unit used to measure liquids

nickel   page 113

5 cents

meter   page 169

a metric unit of measurement that equals 100 centimeters

10   20   30   40   50   60   70   80   90   100

number   page 13

a word that tells how many

 = five

numeral page 13
a symbol that stands for a number

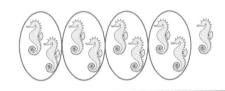 = five = ⑤

penny page 113
1 cent

odd number page 26
a number that cannot be divided into sets of two without a leftover

pint page 175
an amount equal to two cups

oval page 37
a round shape that is longer one way than the other

⬭

place value page 133
the value of a digit depending on its place in a number

hundreds → 532 ← ones
↑
tens

pattern page 9
a series that repeats over and over

A B C A B C A B C

plus page 65
added to

5   ⊕   3   =   8

pound page 180

a customary unit used to measure weight

rectangle page 33

a shape with four sides and four square corners

probability page 339

the chance that something might happen

rhombus page 35

a shape with four equal sides and four corners that are not always square corners

quart page 175

an amount equal to two pints

set page 5

a group of things that are alike in some way

quarter page 119

25 cents

square page 33

a rectangle with four sides that are all the same length

subtract

page 69

to take away

5 − 3 = 2

triangle

page 33

a shape with three sides

sum

page 65

the result of adding two or more numbers

2 + 3 = 5

Venn diagram

page 285

a picture that uses circles to show how sets are alike or different

third

page 227

one part of a whole that has been divided into three equal parts

yard

page 167

a customary unit of measurement that equals 3 feet or 36 inches

1 foot   2 feet   3 feet

trapezoid

page 35

a four-sided figure with no more than two slanted sides